# Eliminate Income Tax

*Form an Unincorporated Nonprofit Association*

KIRK CARMICHAEL

IS B N 978-1-969201-73-8

## *Disclaimer*

This book is for educational purposes only and should not be construed as tax, legal, or financial advice. The readers accept all responsibility for the use or misuse of this material.

# *Dedication*

*This book and ministry are dedicated to the LORD Jesus Christ, Yeshua Ha Mashiach. It is only by His Divine timing and grace that I was me to discover hidden truths of our economic system.*

*Like nearly every young American teenager, I began having income taxes withheld from every paycheck when I got my first job. Nobody questioned it. The assumed income tax cycle continued for the first 38 years of my life, until I was led to assemble the puzzle of how income taxes work, why they are withheld, and why nobody questions the system. Only God can lead a person into truth, and only He can give a person revelation. Being revealed the truth and walking in it can only do one thing: set you free.*

# *Author's Note*

To all governmental entities and media professionals:

This book is written in accordance with the rule of law and the principles of the United States of America. The author aims to observe the Constitution and its provisions relating to freedom and liberty.

This document does not express identification as an enemy combatant or opposition to the government. It communicates support for governmental operations within lawful and constitutional parameters. It notes opposition to governmental actions viewed as overreach or contrary to established standards. The purpose of this work is to explain the lawful framework created by Congress that relates to the exercise of constitutional protections.

This book does not support tax evasion or frivolous tax arguments and should not be seen as providing tax, financial, or legal advice. Its purpose is educational, helping individuals understand their rights under current law without encouraging noncompliance with those to whom it applies. The federal income tax, established in 1913, is lawful, and statutory U.S. citizens residing in the statutory United States are required to pay it. This publication focuses on Americans residing in the 50 states; further clarification is provided within the text for those unfamiliar with this distinction.

Additionally, I have no affiliation with the "sovereign citizen" movement. Nonetheless, I advocate for the principle of individual sovereignty, which reflects the original intentions of our Founding Fathers. This foundational concept informs the framework of our nation, and the present work seeks to advance it in accordance with the law and with due respect.

In conclusion, I recognize that certain elements within government and media may utilize methods such as gaslighting and psychological projection to shape public perception and promote conformity. These tactics aim to deter independent thinking and marginalize dissenting voices. Let it be known that I will respond appropriately to any attempts to discredit myself, my integrity, or the lawful nature of this book through the use of such manipulative techniques.

# Contents

# *Chapter One: A Revelation Of Deception*

It's funny how a single moment can change the way you see everything. I still remember that September in 2009 as if it just happened yesterday. The mortgage crisis was unraveling across the world, with families losing their homes left and right. It was chaos, but at the time, I was doing fine, at least on the surface. I owned a $3 million property, and I had built a good life. It seemed to me as if I understood how the system worked.

Then, something happened that shook me to the core. A friend of mine, Ken, an older man I knew from church, was losing his house to foreclosure. Ken was a casualty caused by the "mortgage crisis" of 2008. Ken wasn't just a friend; he was a good, humble man who didn't deserve the kind of hardship he was going through, and I wanted to help him. I couldn't stand back and watch him lose his home.

"Ken, we're going to figure this out. There has to be a solution." I told him, not sure whether there was even a solution.

So, I started digging. I remember sitting at my computer late into the night, searching the internet for answers, hoping to find something that could help Ken save his home. That's when I stumbled upon something that made me stop in my tracks. There was this guy teaching something I had never heard before: "Banks don't loan money."

I froze. What? Banks don't loan money? That didn't make any sense to me at first. How could that even be true? But this guy, the way he spoke, the way he explained things, he made it sound like he knew exactly what he was talking about. My curiosity turned into something deeper. I had to know more. I couldn't ignore it. I needed to hear him out.

I checked his schedule, and there it was: he was hosting a seminar in Baltimore, Maryland, that very next weekend. Without hesitation, I decided we had to go. I booked two plane tickets, one for me and one for Ken, and covered everything: the flights, the hotel, and the full seminar costs. I wasn't going to leave Ken to deal with this alone.

That weekend changed everything.

It was a three-day seminar held on Friday, Saturday, and Sunday, and I'll never forget what I learned there. I walked into that room believing the system was what it said it was. By the time I walked out, my entire understanding of how things worked had been flipped upside down.

That's when I learned the truth about the Federal Reserve. It hit me like a punch to the gut: The Federal Reserve isn't part of our government at all. It's a private organization controlled by private bankers. In 1913, these bankers conspired with President Woodrow Wilson to take over America's money system. That's when the Federal

Reserve Act was passed. And that's when our country gave up control of its own currency.

Here's how it works, in plain terms: The Federal Reserve prints money out of thin air. It doesn't come from gold, it doesn't come from assets, nothing. They print it and loan it to our government, the U.S. Treasury. And then they charge us, the American people, interest for the privilege of using our own money. Can you imagine how insane that sounds? Our U.S. Treasury, which should be responsible for our nation's money, no longer prints it. The Federal Reserve does. And in doing so, they create debt. Endless debt. And what's worse? The IRS exists to collect that debt. That's their whole function: to collect the interest we owe to these private bankers. There are a lot more details to the history of what took place, which I will cover in a later chapter.

By the end of the seminar, I sat there in disbelief. I couldn't stop shaking my head. My mind was racing, thinking back to everything I thought I knew. I looked at Ken. I could tell he felt it too, that weight, that realization that the system we trusted all our lives had been built on fraud.

On that Sunday evening, as the seminar wrapped up, I sat on the flight back home feeling like a different person. I couldn't unlearn what I had learned. I couldn't pretend I didn't know. The instant I discovered the system's fraud, I changed the way I saw everything.

And that's when I started asking the hard questions. Why don't we print our own money anymore? Who's really in control here?

It wasn't just about Ken anymore. It was about all of us.

When I began digging into the system, it was like falling into a rabbit hole. The deeper I went, the more I uncovered, and the more my faith in what I had believed began to crumble. One of the biggest realizations came during my ongoing research: the truth about the 16th Amendment.

At first, I didn't understand it. The 16th Amendment was supposed to authorize the government to collect income tax, but what I discovered blew me away. There were serious questions about its legitimacy and its limited scope. And I wasn't the only one saying this. I found resource after resource: books, legal papers, videos, and interviews, which laid it all out. It wasn't just a conspiracy theory; it was documented history, and anyone willing to look could see it.

I've spent years gathering those resources, real evidence from credible sources, and I don't keep it to myself. I've shared it with anyone willing to listen, and I'll continue to do so. If someone wants to know, I'm happy to give them the full list. People deserve to know the truth about the system we live in, even if that truth is hard to accept.

Discovering these truths didn't come without its cost. It wasn't just an intellectual realization; it was emotional, too.

I had spent years of my life working hard, building a career, and making real money. At my peak, I was earning nearly a million dollars a year. I had been giving away my money, donating it, really, to a cause I didn't approve of, to a system I didn't believe in.

Imagine working so hard for something, believing you're doing the right thing, only to find out that you've been playing a game where the rules were not fully disclosed to you from the start. That's what it felt like. Decades of deception, all crashing down on me.

But amidst the anger and the confusion, my faith kept me

grounded. I've always believed that God gives us clarity when we need it most. And in that instant of awakening, I heard Him telling me, "You can't keep doing this. You can't keep supporting this system."

It wasn't just about the money anymore. It was about standing for what I believed was right. I knew I couldn't keep paying into something I knew, deep down, was unjust. My faith in God gave me the courage to say, "Enough."

And that's the thing about an awakening. It makes you question everything you've been taught. It stirs up emotions you didn't even know you had. But at the same time, it sets you free.

When I decided to find a solution never to pay income tax again, it wasn't just a rebellious decision; it was a faith-based one. My journey to God was what gave me the clarity and courage to take that step. I held onto a scripture that has always spoken to me: "Jesus is the way, the truth, and the life." That line stayed in my mind because it reminded me of something profound: Jesus is the truth.

I began to process everything I was learning through this lens: if Jesus is the truth, then my life should align with truth, no matter what. And here I was, looking at a system that was built on lies. If the Federal Reserve, the IRS, and the entire financial structure operated in deception, then I couldn't, in good conscience, not learn of new ways to navigate commerce.

I remember telling myself, "If this is a lie, I don't have anything to fear. Even though it's scary, I'll trust that God will lead me to the truth."

Here's what I realized: if Jesus is the truth, then all lies come from Satan. I wasn't going to keep donating my money to something I now saw as fundamentally wrong. It felt like I was funding darkness, and I refused to keep playing that role.

I believe this was my Abrahamic moment of testing my faith. If you've read Genesis, you'll know what I mean. God tested Abraham by asking him to sacrifice his only son, Isaac. It didn't make sense; Isaac was the promised son through whom God had promised Abraham an entire nation. Abraham didn't understand, but he obeyed. He was ready to raise that spear, trusting God even in confusion. And it was at that very moment, when Abraham's faith was proven, that God said, "Stop. Now I know I can trust you."

That's exactly how I felt when I decided to stop contributing to the income tax system. I reached a point where I said, "I don't care if I go to jail. I'm not afraid anymore. I trust God." I believed He would guide me to the truth, and He did. It took a couple of months, but before the year was even over, He had already given me the solution.

Of course, the road to understanding the system wasn't smooth. I didn't just wake up one day and figure it all out. I stumbled a lot. I made mistakes. But here's the thing: the best way to learn something is by getting it wrong first.

In those early days, my zeal often outpaced my knowledge. I was passionate, but I didn't always have the whole picture. I learned the hard way that when the IRS sends you a notice in the mail, you don't just toss it in the trash and say, "Hell with you guys!" That's precisely what I used to do. I thought I was standing up to them, but I didn't realize the IRS is just an accounting system. It's an administrative process. Therefore, by not responding to the notices properly within 30 days, I was actually agreeing to their request. My acquiescence to their notices became my acceptance of their request.

It took time and a lot of trial and error for me to see the structure of what it was. The IRS operates like a bookkeeping service. Their job is to send notices, tally numbers, and keep the process moving. The notices they sent are because the IRS shows there is a liability that we have willfully caused ourselves. The notices aren't personal attacks; they're just part of the machine. And ignoring them without addressing the issues properly only makes things worse.

Looking back now, I'm grateful for the mistakes I made. Those hard lessons taught me the right way to navigate the system. Now, when I help people, I can steer them away from the pitfalls I fell into. I know how to guide someone to safety, step by step, because I've already walked that rocky road.

As I dug deeper into the IRS and the tax system, I began to see something clearly: compliance is built on misunderstanding and fear. It's not just about laws; it's about the confusion that those laws create. The IRS uses a particular kind of language where words don't mean what we think they mean. Take words like "income," "employee," or even "U.S. Citizen." You and I think we know what those terms mean, but the IRS defines them differently. It's almost as if they've created a second language, one that works against the average person who doesn't know how to decode it.

And here's the kicker: It's not just the law itself that matters; it's the intent behind the law. This is where I had an epiphany.

I came across the Congressional record from 1909 when President Taft first introduced the idea of an income tax. I still have that document, and I show it to anyone who's willing to listen. In it, Taft clearly states that the intent of the 16th Amendment was to levy a tax on the National Government. It wasn't meant for the average person. It applies specifically to residents of Washington, D.C., and all people working for the federal government.

So, then, why are we all paying income tax?

It's because of contract law. People unknowingly enter into a contract with the IRS. By signing certain documents, documents most of us don't even fully understand, they agree to things they're unaware of. They agree to pay taxes, they admit to being residents of Washington, D.C. (even if they've never set foot there), and they get locked into a system they never intended to join.

It was this realization that shook me to the core. I began to see how mass confusion and fear keep people compliant. They don't question the system because they don't know where to start. But once you see the cracks in the foundation, you can't unseen them.

Around this same time, I stumbled onto something that would change everything: unincorporated associations. This is what the real deal is. It happened because of that Abrahamic moment I talked about earlier when I said, "I don't care if I go to jail." I had just come back home from that life-changing seminar, and I knew I couldn't keep this to myself.

So, I did what any natural leader would do: I started sharing the information. I had a $3 million property back then, and I began inviting everyone I knew: friends, neighbors, and even strangers. I said, "Bring anyone who wants to hear this. Bring anyone looking for answers."

It was at one of those early meetings that I met a man who would forever change my perspective. He'd been working with unincorporated associations since the 1980s. He sat me down and explained what they were, how they worked, and, most importantly, how they protected people. He told me they had no tax liability.

I didn't need a second opinion.

At the time, I didn't have all the facts or even a deep understanding of what an unincorporated association was. All I knew was that this man had been using them successfully for decades, and that was good enough for me. I told him right then, "I need you to help me set one of these up."

And that's exactly what he did. Over the next several years, I didn't just stop at one, and I set up about fifteen of them.

What's important here is this: I started on faith alone. I believed what he told me. That's it. I didn't have a manual, I didn't have decades of experience, and I didn't have all the answers yet. But I believed.

And in the beginning, that's all you need, faith. Faith that there's a better way, faith that the truth exists, and faith that you'll find it if you keep going.

Over the last fifteen years, I've learned so much more, exponentially more, about unincorporated associations and the system itself. I've studied, researched, and built my understanding piece by piece. But when I started, it wasn't about having every piece of the puzzle. It was about trust.

I trusted God. I trusted the process. And I trusted that I was on the right path.

At the start of this journey, I didn't have a big plan or long-term vision. I wasn't trying to dismantle an entire system or make some grand statement. I was just trying to avoid the IRS and eliminate my personal tax liability. That's it.

At the time, I was running a transportation company that was doing multimillions in sales revenue a year. The only thing on my mind was protecting my income and my assets from a tax I knew I didn't owe. What I didn't realize back then was that my ignorance, the same ignorance that made me throw away IRS letters, was about to teach me some of the most valuable lessons of my life.

See, the IRS operates through contracts. When they send you those letters, they're not just making a request; they're sending you an offer to contract. Here's how it works: If you don't respond to the letter, they take your silence as acceptance.

Since everyone seems to be talking about pickleball these days, let me explain it this way: imagine you're on the court, and someone serves you the ball. If you don't hit it back, what happens? They get the point. It's the same with the IRS. When they send you that letter, and you ignore it, when you don't "hit the ball back," they win. They get your agreement.

That's the trick. You don't even have to write something complicated. You could say, "I don't agree," and it changes everything. At least you've hit the ball back.

For a long time, I didn't hit the ball back. I just kept throwing their notices in the trash, thinking that if I ignored them long enough, they'd go away. They didn't.

The letters turned into phone calls. The phone calls turned into visits. IRS agents started showing up at my house and my business. That's when the fear really set in, not just for me but for my wife. I wasn't just fighting my own fear anymore. I watched the woman I love carry the weight of everything she didn't understand.

So, how did I overcome it? I just kept repeating the truth to myself: The tax doesn't apply to me. The tax doesn't apply to me. And... since this is true, then I will prevail. Over and over again.

But here's the most crucial part: The association I established saved me. They protected me because it allowed me to move all of my assets out of my Social Security number and stopped the yearly reporting. And, because I wasn't receiving any reporting to my Social Security number, I was also able to stop the signing of the annual tax return contracts, which are designed for you to admit you have a tax liability, contractually binding you to the numbers you stated on the contract.

That nine-digit number the government gave you at birth? That's what I call your tracking number. From the day you're born to the day you die, that number follows you. It's the number that you contractually agree to be liable for reporting to the IRS once you begin the cycle of signing tax return contracts.

But what happens if you stop using that number? What happens if you move everything, your money, your properties, your investments, out of that number?

You become a ghost.

That's exactly what I did. I moved everything out of my name and out of my Social Security number. The IRS couldn't find a thing. No bank accounts. No stock accounts. No real estate. Nothing. There was no evidence that I had ever received anything.

And that's when the fear turned into freedom.

After my associations sold the transportation company to my partner in 2020, I found myself searching for something more. I had been successful, sure, saving $200,000 a year in taxes alone, but I wasn't fulfilled. I needed meaning. I needed purpose.

It was in prayer that the memory of my spiritual deliverance from the satanic deception of the tax system resurfaced. This journey wasn't just financial; it was about breaking free from a system that I now believed to be deeply flawed. I realized I had to help others find their way out, too. It wasn't enough for me to keep this knowledge to myself; I had been delivered, and it was my turn to provide for others. That's when I formed UnincorporatedAssociations.com, a platform designed to educate and equip people with the tools, documentation, and understanding they need to set up their own associations and become tax-exempt.

Here's the most important lesson I share with people: The IRS is not out to get you. They're not following you. They're not listening to your calls. They're not tracking you with GPS.

At one point, I was teaching about associations in a live classroom setting, and a man asked a question that sounded like he thought the IRS was chasing him down the street, peeking into his rearview mirror. I stopped and said, "Friend, they don't care about you like that."

Here's the truth: The IRS isn't some shadowy monster. They're not bullies. What they care about is accounting. It's a game of numbers. When you use an association, you remove your assets and income from your name. You don't technically earn anything anymore, so they never expect a tax return from you in the first place. There's nothing to fear if you understand how the system works.

This all comes back to a biblical principle. In the Book of Hosea, God says: "My people are destroyed for a lack of knowledge."

We live in a world full of fear and deception, and it's that lack of understanding that keeps us in chains. People file their tax returns because they think they have to. They believe that if they don't, the IRS will come after them. But here's the irony: filing the return is what creates the liability in the first place.

Think about it. When you file a tax return, you're signing a legal contract under penalty of perjury. By signing it, you're saying:

"Yes, I agree. I owe this tax. And if I'm lying, I agree to go to jail."

It's madness. People fear not filing, when it's the very act of filing that traps them.

My journey started as a personal fight to save my business and protect my assets. But today, it's about so much more. It's about helping people wake up to the truth, about empowering them with knowledge so they can break free from fear and deception.

The IRS isn't a monster. It's a system. And like any system, it can be understood and navigated. My mission is to share what I've learned and to show others that freedom is possible. You don't have to be a slave to a system designed to take captive all uneducated Americans. You just need the courage to seek the truth and the knowledge to act on it.

# *Chapter Two: Overcoming Fear And Misinformation*

The IRS doesn't scam you outright—they don't have to. The genius of the system lies in how it convinces you that blind compliance is your duty, even though most people know or at least have heard that there are problems with the system. Let me begin by elaborating further on how the IRS falls under 'implied responsibility' and how very few people question the system until they are informed that they have never even owed the tax. Paying taxes to the IRS is part of your social contract. Wrong!

So, I graduated from college in 1993 and worked as an employee for a company until 1999. During that time, taxes were straightforward for me: fixed deductions came out of my paycheck, and I didn't question it. Because that's just how it is, right? I didn't know any better. I just consistently received my paycheck every week and never questioned the deductions as to why and what they were for. I received the same exact amount each week and had the same amount deducted for taxes. I had believed the entire time of my employment as a W-2 employee that I could not control the tax deductions that my employer was withholding (and forwarding to the IRS on my behalf) out of my paycheck. Things began to change when I started my own business in 1999. I was no longer an employee but the owner of a business. Now, there were taxes to be paid both for the company and for me personally. That's when I began to notice how arbitrary the system seemed. There was no apparent logic or standard approach to why I owed specific amounts. The deductions and calculations were based on various factors that did not always make sense. In fact, they rarely made any sense.

When I hired an accountant, I was asked questions like, "Do you have a home office?" or "How many miles do you drive a year?" These questions felt utterly unrelated to my work as a freight broker and the owner of a transportation company. It started to become evident to me that the system was more like a game to figure out how to minimize the taxes owed rather than following any clear, rational guidelines. In retrospect, I see this was the first step in taking note of what seemed problematic with the system. I remained in an "implied responsible" state of mind, awaiting the moment in time at the seminar in Baltimore, MD, in September of 2009, when everything would change. Maybe this book will be that moment for you.

From 1999 to 2009, I was still operating in a "zombie-like" state, handing over receipts and bank statements to my accountant for him to wave a magic wand over the contract he would later have me sign and advise the check I needed to cut to the IRS. Every year, she aimed to reduce my tax burden as much as possible, but it always gave me the feeling that I was paying a significant amount of money for reasons I didn't fully understand, nor did I ever investigate. I saw the fingerprints of the problematic system everywhere, but didn't question it deeply.

Then, in 2009, I had what I can only describe as an awakening. I realized that the tax system itself was built on deception. Most people, including me, entered the tax system unknowingly by signing a contract, a private agreement with the IRS. In case you didn't fully understand this last statement, let me restate: most Americans do not owe the Federal Income tax from birth, but rather they opt into being labeled a taxpayer when they sign their first 1040 tax return under penalty of perjury. The contract makes them liable, and not the 16th Amendment, which is the authority of the federal income tax. There is a difference between the authority of the Federal Income tax initiated by the 16th Amendment, signed into law in February of 1913, and being subject to the jurisdiction of the tax. It was eye-opening to discover that most Americans have never owed Federal Income tax from birth (or entry into America on a visa) simply because they do not live in Washington, D.C., or work for the Federal Government as a federal employee. Instead, they owe taxes because they voluntarily signed a 1040 tax contract, albeit by deceit, agreeing to be labeled as taxpayers.

This realization reframed my entire understanding of the system. The arbitrary deductions, the endless forms, and the complexity of the process all began to make sense when viewed as a game designed to keep people compliant and uninformed.

I'll explain this 'deception' in detail moving forward, and I guarantee you will be shocked to learn that the system is not as it appears. This is a critical point that needs to be laid out clearly so others can see the truth for themselves.

Since I had nobody to help me through the process of eliminating tax liability and what it means to stop cold turkey from filing any more 1040 tax contracts, I did everything the wrong way at first. My zeal to never pay another dollar to the system led my path to where I am now with no tax liability, but for the first several years, I still had things to learn about how to make simple moves to avoid tax liability, which would have saved me some hassle along the way.

After I stopped filing 1040 tax returns, I started throwing collection notices straight into the trash, which, as I stated in the last chapter, was the worst thing I could have done. When the IRS mails a notice addressing your social security account (they are mailing it to you as an authorized representative of the account), they send a request to settle a discrepancy in their accounting system. By not responding to them at all in 30 days, they accept their request as your acceptance and begin an administrative action, which, with no responses to their letters, eventually ends in them filing a Lien and then a Levy against the Social Security account and all assets held in that 9-digit number. To avoid collection activity by the IRS from your social security account, there is a simple way to remove yourself from the IRS' jurisdiction. I still had to learn to do it. However, keeping your social security account under the jurisdiction of the IRS and not addressing their notices in a timely manner may result in a seemingly relentless attempt to assess and collect the debt they are trying to get you to agree to.

When I made the vow to God that I wasn't going to pay another dollar because I knew I didn't owe it, I thought that was enough. But it wasn't. Originally, I didn't have any solutions, and I was still in harm's way (perceived harm's way). For two or three months, I had no direction other than my determination not to pay. That period was chaotic, and the lack of a clear plan left me vulnerable.

My first step in eliminating tax liability changed when I had what I call a divine appointment. I met someone who introduced me to strategies revolving around the formation of an entity called an unincorporated nonprofit association, which completely shifted my understanding of what it means to eliminate tax liability. These associations became the tools I've relied on ever since. These unincorporated nonprofit associations are not associated with any individual social security number. That knowledge and approach became the foundation for moving forward in a way that aligned with what I had later learned regarding the 16th Amendment and the limited jurisdiction of the IRS.

It's a lesson in how misinformation, or better yet, no truthful information whatsoever, and myths influenced my decisions for many years, but also how truth brings clarity and how the right tool helped me change course.

Most people fear the IRS because they associate it with stories of people going to jail, like Wesley Snipes. The fear is deeply emotional; nobody wants to go to jail, so they'll do anything to avoid it. The problem is that this fear often paralyzes people or leads them to mindlessly comply with the system without understanding it. There is a reason people go to jail, and it always involves two components;

1. Filing a tax return contract under penalty of perjury, waiving your constitutionally protected rights (yes, believe it or not, the US Constitution actually protects you from a direct tax from the Federal government), and

2. Maliciously and intentionally misreporting the amounts you have agreed by contract that were received by your social security number in a given year, which the IRS shows as a greater amount reported.

A perfect example of misguided fear by using a person like Wesley Snipes, going to jail is this... Wesley Snipes not only signed a tax return, but in protesting the tax system, he actually signed a tax contract under penalty of perjury, claiming that the IRS owed him a $7.5-million refund.

Can you see how this is a unique circumstance where Mr. Snipes literally hung himself? Did he owe taxes? Yes, but ONLY because he signed a contract with the IRS. Did the IRS owe him 7.5 million dollars back to him? No! All the years prior, Mr. Snipes had been filing tax contracts, admitting to the numbers he had signed under penalty of perjury. Just because he discovers later, he doesn't owe the money, he still agrees by his signature all the years prior.

Here's what I've observed: People assume that once the IRS is involved, they have no options. They see themselves as powerless because they lack knowledge about how the system works. They don't understand what creates a tax liability or how to avoid it. Instead, they believe their only choices are to pay whatever they're told they owe or risk punishment. Furthermore, they run to people with licenses (such as CPAs or tax attorneys) whose job is to keep them in a contractual relationship with the IRS, and the vicious cycle of tax liability only continues.

And, as another reminder... this annual filing of tax contracts only keeps a person in harm's way and liable to the contract you are signing, just like Wesley Snipes, who first signed a tax return under penalty of perjury, creating a liability. Then, he made things worse by claiming the IRS owed him $7.5 million. These actions put him in harm's way, and his lack of understanding of how the system operates sealed his fate.

When people bring up Wesley Snipes, I always ask: "Do you know why he went to jail, or do you just know that he did?" Most don't know the details. This lack of information feeds their fear, leading them to comply without question, of which even a vast majority of people have never owed the tax.

Did you know that there are approximately 350 million Americans? Of the 350 million Americans, you being one of them, do you know how many people were charged with a tax crime in the year 2022? The answer is: 2300 people. Mathematically speaking, that's .000006% of people, or 1 in every 152,000 people. And, of the 2300 tax crimes brought to Court in the year 2022, 2200 of the 2300 cases involved tax filers, people who consistently signed yearly contracts under penalty of perjury with the IRS. The remaining 100 were nontax filers with extenuating circumstances.

Now, at least 1/3 of Americans don't even file a yearly tax return. That means that approximately 200 million Americans are blindly filing tax returns and voluntarily paying a percentage of their earnings, yet they have never even owed the tax or been subject to the 16th Amendment. Misguided perception with fear as a motivator is the culprit for robbing a majority of wealth from our Country and fueling some evil agendas with the donations.

The fear of the IRS is like being stuck in a rowboat in the middle of the ocean. You hear on the radio that a storm is coming, and panic sets in. But without any sense of direction, you don't know which way to row. Out of fear, you might start rowing aimlessly or, worse, row in the direction of the storm. Fear drives people to act without understanding or to avoid action altogether, leaving them vulnerable.

This fear-based approach is what keeps people trapped. They don't ask questions, don't seek knowledge, and don't take control of their situation. Instead, they become blind slaves to the system, paying taxes they most likely have never owed because they fear unknown consequences.

The mental shift from fear to confidence in financial matters, mainly when dealing with the IRS, begins with understanding the facts and challenging misconceptions. Most people operate out of fear because they don't know their rights or the limits of the IRS's authority.

To make this mental shift, individuals must start by educating themselves and challenging the myths that perpetuate unnecessary anxiety.

Here's how they can take the first steps toward empowerment:

You see, understanding the historical facts is crucial. For example, over 98% of Americans have never owed federal income tax since birth. The IRS's jurisdiction is extremely limited to Washington, D.C. If you don't live in Washington, D.C. or work for the Federal Government based in Washington, D.C., then the tax doesn't inherently apply to you. The only reason you carry tax liability is because you have voluntarily signed a 1040 tax contract agreeing to be taxed as if you lived in Washington, D.C.

Another key part of overcoming fear is understanding what jurisdiction means. Jurisdiction determines the authority an entity has over you. For instance, if you live in the U.S., you're not concerned about the Mexican government raiding your bank account or any of the laws they pass. Why? Because Mexico has no jurisdiction over Americans or American banks. Similarly, the IRS is not a government agency like the FBI or CIA. The IRS is not a governmental entity! While it functions as a collection agency for the U.S. Treasury (a governmental agency), it was primarily created in 1913 to collect interest on the national debt for the Federal Reserve, another non-governmental entity given authority via a law signed ten months after the 16th Amendment was passed in December.

In 1913, the 16th Amendment to the U.S. Constitution was ratified, granting Congress the authority to impose a federal income tax, but this authority was limited to be only on the National Government based in Washington, D.C., including anybody living there or working from there, but the well-planned agenda was to put the tax in place and create a reason for people to voluntarily pay it by creating an illusion of a "national debt".

When you understand that the IRS's jurisdiction is limited and that its authority over you is only granted through your signing and agreeing to voluntary contracts, you start to see that its power isn't as all-encompassing as it's often perceived. Another myth is that they are looking into your life arbitrarily, following your financial activity, or listening to your phone calls. They don't have to! The system is truly voluntary, and they know that most people continually volunteer to donate money they never owed.

You know how they say fear thrives in the absence of knowledge. People often panic because they assume the IRS can do whatever it wants. But when you fully understand the principle of jurisdiction and why you have lost jurisdiction voluntarily, their authority is not as vast as it appears. For example, if you haven't signed a tax return under penalty of perjury in a given year, you haven't entered into a contract agreeing that you owe a specific amount. The worst that happens is that you receive a request to file your yearly contract they have been receiving from you in a year that they show you received money. They cannot access a tax liability on you without you agreeing to the amount by signing the return. They can, however, continue an administrative process against you if you do not reply to their requests. We will cover this in a later chapter.

By using an unincorporated nonprofit association to receive money or assets, your Social Security number stops having money reported to the IRS. Then, each year, you have no reporting to your social security number, and no tax return contract is expected to be signed—end of story.

Confidence comes from being informed. It is invaluable to have someone who can explain these concepts and walk you through the process. Visual analogies, like the comparison between the IRS and foreign governments, help make these ideas clear and relatable.

Ultimately, the shift to confidence requires a mindset change. Recognize that your fear is often based on misunderstanding or misinformation. Once you're equipped with the truth, you can make decisions that align with your understanding, not just react out of fear.

There are certain steps you can take to avoid entering into a contractual agreement with the IRS, thereby eliminating their oversight and potential liability. One step is to send a formal notice, called a Revocation of Election, to the IRS stating that you do not reside in Washington, D.C., which is the key aspect of their jurisdiction. An additional step is to stop receiving money reported to your Social Security number.

The IRS tracks every dollar reported by other entities for which you received money under your Social Security number, so when you take the step to remove reporting from entities you do business with to your Social Security number, the solution lies in structuring your financial affairs differently. By using an unincorporated nonprofit association, you can remove your Social Security number from your financial operations. You could even transfer ownership of a business to the association instead of having your Social Security number own the company directly.

******

Curious about more sources of information regarding the tax system? Let me introduce you to someone you've likely never heard of—Joe Bannister. You can find his testimony on YouTube. Once an esteemed member of the IRS Criminal Investigative Division, Joe carried a badge, wielded a gun, and arrested individuals who failed to pay their taxes. His role was clear-cut, and he believed wholeheartedly in the mandatory nature of taxes. However, his perspective began to shift after an incident that challenged his understanding.

One day, while listening to a talk show on a San Francisco radio station, the topic of discussion was that taxes are voluntary, not mandatory. At first, Joe dismissed the claim, thinking that it can't be true; I carry a gun and arrest people over taxes. Yet, the statement lingered in his mind, gnawing at his sense of duty and understanding.

Being an honorable man with a strong commitment to truth, Joe decided to investigate the matter further. For two years, during nights and weekends, he conducted extensive research. His work culminated in a 50-page report in which he meticulously itemized all the laws, statutes, and codes related to income taxes. His findings were shocking: not a single law required a majority of American citizens to file and pay an income tax return. I have a copy of his 50-page report, which he put together after two years of research on his daily job.

Joe's revelations are not unique. Many others have uncovered similar truths, shared testimonies, and created informational resources. These pioneers in the field have laid a foundation for understanding the tax system in a new light. Do you get it now? Do you see how blatantly you are being ripped off of YOUR money? In the end, you will have nobody to blame but yourself, but take it easy on yourself. It all occurred through deception.

Preparation plays a crucial role in overcoming fear and uncertainty when dealing with these matters. The first step is to assess your current situation, including identifying the last year you filed a tax return contract, understanding what year you are currently in, and determining how much money you have been receiving under your Social Security number. This provides clarity on where you stand and what needs to be addressed.

Once the assessment is complete, the next step is to develop a plan to reorganize your financial affairs. This plan would involve transitioning the receipt of money from your Social Security number to an unincorporated Nonprofit Association, which is not subject to the jurisdiction of the IRS. This change eliminates future interactions with the IRS and eliminates personal liability.

Addressing any existing tax liabilities before transitioning to the association may be important for individuals who want to avoid any hassle with the IRS. This may involve filing outstanding tax returns and paying any taxes owed based on prior agreements. While this step can be taken after moving into the associations, even though you most likely have never owed the tax, to begin with, you can sign the last contracts and wrap up the accounting reported to the IRS. If you can stand on the truth of not owing the tax, sending correspondence to the

IRS addressing your nontaxpayer status is also a viable option. Just know that either approach is dependent on your own personal faith in the truth you are now discovering, and that everything is voluntary.

Let me give you two examples of individuals who overcame their fear and took control of their finances by making informed decisions:

A couple from Florida had not filed their 2023 tax return and were uncertain about how to proceed. They were guided on sending a specific letter to the IRS while simultaneously establishing an association. The letter was, as stated before, a "Revocation of Election." They also effectively reorganized their financial structure by moving their assets from personal ownership into the association. About 10 months after sending the letter, they received an acknowledgment from the IRS stating that their 2023 tax obligations were satisfied without them having to file a tax contract or pay any association admissions. This resolution brought them significant relief and confidence.

Another case involved a husband and wife in Missouri facing a $75,000 tax liability from a property investment in 2022. They discovered this approach just in time, on October 15th, the deadline for filing their taxes. By forming an association, they were able to address the liability through reassignment, effectively eliminating the $75,000 tax burden. This proactive step resolved their immediate concern and gave them greater control over their financial future.

For anyone feeling overwhelmed by the fear of the IRS, the first step is understanding the history of taxation, which we'll explore shortly. It's essential to grasp the foundations of the system, including why tax liabilities exist in the first place.

A key point to remember is that when the IRS addresses you, they aren't talking to your physical self. Instead, they address the Social Security number assigned to you at birth or when you moved to the United States. This number represents a fictitious entity that mirrors your name, and you are the authorized representative of that account. When you sign documents or tax returns, you are not signing on behalf of yourself as a person but as the representative of the Social Security account. The IRS is not pursuing you as an individual; they are addressing the tax liability related to that entity. Understanding this distinction can greatly reduce fear and help you focus on resolving the liability tied to that account.

By educating yourself on these key points and recognizing the true nature of the IRS's actions, you can shift your mindset and gain control over the situation.

Fear loses its grip when replaced by knowledge, and with the right strategies, perspective, and support, anyone can take control of their financial reality, stepping away from blind compliance into informed empowerment. This shift—from fear to understanding—is the first step toward challenging the system and protecting your rights.

# *Chapter Three: The Legal Foundation Of Freedom*

Let's discuss these associations, which are unincorporated. In the next couple of chapters, we discuss in detail how the 'Federal' Income Tax, when passed into law in February 1913, was a tax on the 'Federal' (National) Government itself and not on the individual States and their citizens. In other words, the jurisdiction of this tax extended only to the 10-square-mile area of Washington, D.C. and to federal government agencies. I hope you can see within the definition itself that 'Federal' Income Tax refers to the 'Federal' Government. This law has never changed.

The reason people who do not live in Washington, D.C. or work for a government agency owe Federal Income Tax is that they filed a tax return (essentially a contract) with the IRS, thereby agreeing to the jurisdiction and the tax. The 1040 tax return, required to be filed on April 15 each year, is a contract you may choose to sign or not. Once signed, you agree that the tax for that year applies to you.

As absurd as it sounds, by signing, you are continually agreeing that you live in Washington, D.C., and/or work for the Army or Navy (federal government).

So, continuing with this unincorporated definition, the IRS defines 'THE UNITED STATES' as the territory of Washington, D.C., which is created as a legal fiction intended to deceive the population. A legal fiction is a corporation. Yes, when you or I hear the phrase 'United States,' we assume it refers to the 50 physical states where we reside, but in the IRS tax manual, it is defined exclusively to mean Washington, D.C.

To be 'unincorporated,' as in forming an 'unincorporated association,' is to remain outside the jurisdiction of Washington, D.C., which is a corporation known as 'THE UNITED STATES.'

The legal makeup of an unincorporated association (UA) is that there is no ownership assigned to anybody. No ownership means no personal liability when the UA becomes a legal entity and is registered with the Secretary of State. I know what you may be thinking because we've been trained our entire life to think that we need to own assets in our name, but you see, that's the trap of the system. Even your name, when used in commerce, is a legal fiction — created the day you were born, in the form of your 9-digit Social Security number.

So, while you may think this gives you control being "in your name", you are using the government entity that they set up for you from birth, and are also assigned the liability of owning assets in that 9-digit tracking number (that's my name for it). There is a reason Nelson Rockefeller quoted the famous saying, "The secret to success is to own nothing but control everything". He said this because owning nothing (in your name, aka Social Security number) means owning no liabilities.

So, what's the magic behind this whole thing? It all traces back to the 16th Amendment, the IRS's extremely limited taxing authority. Many people think, "This is too good to be true," but that's only because they've spent a lifetime being programmed to think that the tax applies to them. It's actually "too bad to be true." 98% of Americans have never owed the tax, and yet they think leaving the jurisdiction of the taxing system is "too good to be true."

**Question:** Do you know anyone over the age of 25 who has never filed an income tax return — in other words, never signed a contract with the IRS? If what I'm saying is true, that the Federal Income Tax only applies to people the moment they sign the contract and enter the Federal tax system, then isn't that "too bad to be true"?

The worst part is that most people entered the first contract at a young age, sometimes after their first job, believing it was simply the law they had to follow. In reality, it was their voluntary agreement to a contract. That is definitely "too bad to be true."

Most folks are completely in the dark about this! They stroll through life, completely oblivious that by signing a tax contract with the IRS, they're basically handing over their constitutionally protected rights and willfully donating their hard-earned money.

Now, let's talk about exempt status with the IRS. You must always remember that everybody is exempt from the Federal Income Tax from birth unless they live in Washington, D.C., or begin work for the Federal Government as a Federal employee.

Without this fundamental understanding of the law, the story could get more complicated. Many people associate a tax exemption with that of a religious organization with a 501c (3) status. A lot of faith groups are told they need to fill out an application to be exempt.

When they do, they enter into a contract with the IRS and are given the "privilege" of giving tax-deductible receipts to donors. So, if a person donates to their local church and puts $10,000 in the collection plate, the church will provide them with a receipt at the end of the year for the $10,000 donation, and then they take that receipt as a write-off on their personal yearly tax return contract.

Do you see how the perception of a religious exemption granted by the IRS as a "privilege" to hand out to patrons and requirements that the religious organization follows perpetuates the tax system? Even though the religious organization isn't required to pay taxes, they hand out receipts, empowering the congregants to continue to file tax return contracts by using the donation receipt they received from the church.

My best analogy for the unincorporated nonprofit association and the exemption it receives from the IRS —compared to 501(c)(3) recognized religious organizations, which contract with the IRS to gain their exemption and the "privilege" to issue receipts to donors — is this:

At one time in history, a man could go to the ocean, cast a fishing rod, and pull out a fish freely, under God's economy. Later, however, another man comes along and says to the fisherman, "You know what? From now on, you need a license to fish."

Once a person gives up their God-given right to fish in God's ocean by applying for a license, they can lose the privilege to fish if they lose that license. Religious organizations that apply for exemption by contract with the IRS are in a similar position: they gain the "privilege" to issue tax-deductible receipts, but only by entering into a contract that can restrict or later revoke their rights.

The tax-exempt status of an unincorporated nonprofit association is not a privilege, but a God-given right of private membership, independent of Washington, D.C. This is accomplished through a special registration process that does not tie any individual's Social Security number to ownership of the association.

What does it mean to form an unincorporated nonprofit association? It means you don't have to file a yearly tax report or contract. You won't need to fill out forms each year or worry about whether you've claimed everything correctly. Importantly, you are not being monitored by the IRS yearly, and this arrangement will not trigger a "red flag" for not receiving money under your Social Security number or within a private association.

Again, to emphasize this point, think about a time when all someone had to do was cast a line into the ocean and catch a fish. That fish belonged to no one; it was simply part of the natural order. Then the man-made laws stepped in and said you had to have a license to fish. Associations are fishing in the ocean of commerce with no license needed by virtue of not being under the jurisdiction of Washington, D.C., as most of us from birth have never been.

Being unincorporated means that you're not bound by the statutes and codes governing incorporated entities. The key takeaway here is to stop viewing commercial activity as if it's tied to your personal identity. Instead, recognize that you can operate through any entity you choose, acting as a conduit in commerce. When you sign any business contract, tax document, investment account, or legal agreement, it's crucial to understand that you're not personally obligating yourself. You're acting on behalf of the entity for which you are the authorized user.

This distinction is vital. When you operate outside the confines of your Social Security number, you essentially become a ghost in the world of commerce. This ghostly status allows you to eliminate personal liability. You're not the one on the hook; the entity is. As it relates to taxes, the unincorporated nonprofit association can eliminate personal income tax.

## The Power of the Unincorporated Association

When I think about my early problems, I remember having tax issues in 2009, when I first learned about these ideas. In court, I had to deal with creditors, and I also had to pay taxes that were linked to my SSN. It was hard to be there, but I was able to escape using this ghostly way. Your money can't be taken by the IRS, a court, or creditors if your Social Security number isn't linked to any assets. Thieves of all sorts will not be able to see you anymore.

This shift in perspective changed everything for me. I discovered ways to conduct business that protect my personal assets, and it opened my eyes to possibilities I hadn't considered. It's about understanding the rules and learning how to play the game to your advantage.

Think about a person who is going through a divorce. I once met a dad who was having a hard time paying child support. I'm not saying that people should ignore their duties, but the system can sometimes make things too hard for parents. It can put a lot of stress on the finances, and the courts don't always have many ways to make people pay.

This is where the link comes in handy. The court does not have the legal power to seize any funds that belong to the private group. What this means is that the association stands between the people involved in court judgments, divorce agreements, creditors, and child support. This information is important for people facing legal problems because it shows how a private group can protect its finances.

The organization can also protect its members from different legal claims, such as cases or debtor claims. For instance, if someone is being sued over a business matter, any assets kept in a private group are usually safe from personal responsibility. This means that the person's home, cash, and other personal belongings will be secure even if they lose the case.

# *Chapter Four: The Deception Of The 16th Amendment*

Power doesn't need to be taken by force when people can be convinced to surrender it willingly. The greatest cons in history aren't the ones pulled off in the shadows—they're the ones carried out in plain sight, dressed up as law, necessity, and even patriotism.

The 16th Amendment of 1913 and the Federal Reserve Act of 1913 didn't force Americans into financial servitude overnight. They didn't have to. The true brilliance of the system lies in how it convinced people that taxation on their labor was inevitable, normal, and even their duty. No soldiers marched in. No warnings were given. One day, the people woke up and believed they owed something they never legally did.

As we will discuss in the next chapter, the well-planned agenda infiltrated American households nationwide over decades through the false narrative of a "national debt." The deception we will discuss is that these two combined acts of law (the 16th Amendment and

Federal Reserve Act) were passed through Congress ten months apart from each other, eventually resulting in a successful plan to have people volunteer to pay a tax that they never owed based on a false premise. The plan is so ingenious that it makes the tax seem mandatory after a person opts in by signing their first tax contract at a young age, resulting in never questioning if the tax applies to them and legitimizing the false narrative. We, being the offspring of prior ignorant generations, do not even know what we do not know, causing many to believe the federal income tax is mandatory.

This wasn't just about collecting revenue. This was about control— control of currency, control of policy, and, most importantly, control of the people themselves. For the third time in American history, the banking elite attempted to install a central bank. Unlike the first two failed attempts, this time, they succeeded. And with the 16th Amendment conveniently in place, they could now tax every dollar Americans earned if they believed they owed it, ensuring that the financial system would no longer serve the people but rather the powerful few who created it.

Before 1913, the United States had little to no perpetual national debt. Government funding primarily came from tariffs, duties, and excise taxes, which meant the government had to operate within its means. However, once the Federal Reserve was in place and an income tax was legalized, the debt machine was born. The government could now borrow indefinitely from this new line of credit, which was established through the Federal Reserve Act. The important fundamental principle of the currency system created through the Federal Reserve Act is that our currency became debt-based, meaning that when money that didn't exist, to begin with, is "loaned" to the U.S. Treasury, what happens is the money supply is diluted more and more as the lending continues.

If you've ever wondered about the economic mechanism that causes prices of milk, gasoline, houses, automobiles, etc., to climb over the years (called "inflation"), the scheme that I've just described is the sole factor. This becomes a hidden tax (the Federal Reserve being the beneficiary of) in diluting our money supply, causing the price of a twelve-ounce can of Coke in 1945 to go from .05 cents to $1.95 today. The production process and materials are the same. It's the purchasing power of the dollar that has greatly diminished over time, causing prices to rise because more dollars are needed to buy the same goods and services.

Before we discuss in the next chapter the Federal Reserve Act and the agenda of the "national debt," which passes this increasing hidden tax called "inflation" to Americans, we must speak about how this two-step plan to capture taxation from Americans began with the passing of a tax law, the 16th Amendment.

To understand this better, let's examine how laws are passed. Congress is responsible for drafting and passing legislation, while the President's role is to sign it into law. When the 16th Amendment was proposed, it had to go through Congress and be ratified by the states. Now, put yourself in the position of a congressman in 1913—an elected official representing the people of a sovereign state. Would you have voted for a law that imposed a direct tax on your constituents, knowing that such a tax was both unconstitutional and would not benefit your state? The answer is an astounding NO.

The reality is that the 16th Amendment would not have received a single vote in Congress had it been drafted and voted on to apply to ordinary citizens living in the states. It was very clearly presented to the lawmakers of the time that this amendment to the Constitution did not create a mandatory income tax on all Americans but rather had nothing to do with anybody residing in their states unless the federal government employed them. The general public never really introduced this law, as it went largely unnoticed and had no immediate impact on anybody.

So, if the original understanding of the 16th Amendment was that it didn't apply to the majority of Americans, how did we get to where we are today? That's the key question—one of which I am sure you should be thinking... how are so many people in our generation believing the tax applies to them? To answer this question, it must be understood that there was an agenda put into place that extended past the time of the passing of the underlying law of the federal income tax, the 16th Amendment. It was essential first to put a taxing law in place, and then, over time, they could get people to believe that they owed it.

## The 16$^{th}$ Amendment and the Unconstitutionality of a Direct Tax

You may have heard the phrase "unconstitutional" before. While it may seem elementary for some, and others may not truly grasp what it means to be unconstitutional, it is essential to put the unconstitutionality of a federal income tax on American citizens into its proper perspective. Yes, a mandated federal income tax is unconstitutional. Mandated is the keyword. The federal income tax has seemed mandatory for most because they at one time volunteered and opted into the system. However, the Constitution protects you from having to pay. Here is a quote about why we have a Constitution that protects you against the government.

*The [U.S.] Constitution is a limitation on the government, not on private individuals ... it does not prescribe the conduct of private individuals, only the conduct of the government ... it is not a charter for government power, but a charter of the citizens' protection against the government.*

**—Ayn Rand**

I was surprised when I was first shown that the Constitution has protection from the government against being levied a tax, so no doubt many reading this will be as well. Here is what Article 1, Section 9, Clause 4 of the 1789 Constitution states:

*No capitation or other direct tax shall be laid unless it is in proportion to the Census or enumeration.*

**— Article 1, Section 9, Clause 4 of the Constitution**

What this is saying is that there cannot be a direct tax levied on the American people from the National Government unless it is in proportion to the Census or enumeration. So, now look at the reading of the 16th Amendment and pay attention to the phrase without apportionment:

The Congress shall have power to lay and collect taxes on incomes, from whatever source derived, without apportionment among the several states, and without regard to any census or enumeration – 1913, the 16th Amendment to the Constitution. So, wait a minute! The Constitution protects you from a tax unless it is in proportion to the census or enumeration, but the 16th Amendment is a tax without apportionment! How can the 16th Amendment contradict the Constitution? It doesn't! The 16th Amendment very deceitfully uses the phrase "several states" as to whom it applies. Their use of the phrase "several states" means Washington, D.C., Guam, and Puerto Rico. They did not say "50 states" or "Republic States" for a reason! At any rate, hopefully, you can see there clearly is a contradiction to the 16th

Amendment of the very Constitution by which it was added if it applies to you and to me living outside of Washington, D.C.

In summary, the IRS is a direct tax levied on anybody living in Washington, D.C. or working for the federal government. If this is not you, which it most likely is not, then you are protected by the Constitution from the IRS collecting from you, unless. You opted into the system by signing a 1040 contract with them, which most likely is you as well. You told them that upon the first contract you signed, you lived in Washington, D.C., and were subject to tax without apportionment.

## Congress Members Who Passed the 16th Amendment

To understand how the 16th Amendment became law, it is crucial to know how legislation is passed. The process follows a structured sequence, ensuring that no law is enacted without multiple levels of approval. Below is the step-by-step breakdown of how a bill, including a constitutional amendment, moves through Congress:

1. An idea is conceived: Legislation begins with a proposed idea, often introduced to address a specific issue or perceived need. In the case of the 16th Amendment, the "idea" conceived in 1909 (four years before being passed through Congress) was clear that this was a fundraising effort for the National Government, not a tax on individual state citizens. A bit later in this chapter, we will look at President Taft's own words when presenting this bill in the Congressional record. The push for a federal income tax to tax individual citizens had been attempted over the decades, particularly freshly in everyone's mind was a tax that lasted only one year after being struck down by the Pollock v. Farmers' Loan & Trust Co.

(1895) Supreme Court decision as being unconstitutional, so there was no chance to get approval proposing an income tax in the same way as the past.

2. A representative sponsors a bill containing the idea: A member of Congress drafts and sponsors the bill.

3. The bill is assigned to a committee for study: Congressional committees review and analyze the proposed bill, debating its impact. This stage is critical because committees conduct hearings, survey the value of the bill, gather expert testimony, and determine whether the bill should proceed. To lay a direct tax on individuals residing in the republic states was not only contrary to the constitution, but had the bill been presented as a tax on individual state citizens, and that the money generated would give no economic value in return to the states, the committee would have turned it down before going any further.

4. If released by the committee, the bill is put on a calendar to be voted on. If a committee approves the bill, it is scheduled for debate and voting. At this point, amendments and revisions may be made before it moves forward. There is no chance a committee would have brought the bill this far if it were to tax congressmen's own state citizens.

5. The bill must be approved by the House of Representatives. A simple majority of 218 out of 435 votes is required for passage. In the case of the 16th Amendment, the Senate actually passed the amendment first on July 5, 1909, followed by the House on July 12, 1909. The amendment received overwhelming support in both chambers. At the time, it was widely understood that the taxing authority applied primarily

to residents and entities within federal jurisdiction—namely, Washington, D.C., and federal employees. This is why it came to be referred to as a "federal" income tax—indicating a tax administered by the federal government within its own legal territory and scope.

6. The bill moves to the Senate for majority approval. Although typically the bill proceeds from the House to the Senate. In the case of the 16th Amendment, the Senate took the lead and approved it first. A simple majority of 51 out of 100 votes was required, and the amendment passed the Senate on July 5, 1909. The House followed with its approval on July 12, 1909, and the amendment was ratified on February 3, 1913.

7. A committee is formed to reconcile differences between the House and Senate versions. If changes are made, members from both chambers form a conference committee to unify the final version before sending it back for approval. This ensures both the House and Senate agree on the final language of the bill. There was meticulous examination of this bill through this process that there was no chance at all of getting this far if congressmen were aware their state people were to be taxed and their state would receive no financial benefit.

8. The Government Publishing Office prints the revised bill through a process called enrolling. Once finalized, the official version of the bill is prepared and formally recorded.

9. The President has 10 days to sign or veto the enrolled bill. Once it reaches the President's desk, he can either sign it into law or veto it. However, constitutional amendments follow a different process. Instead of requiring the President's signature, an amendment must be ratified by three-fourths (¾)

of the states. The 16th Amendment was ratified on February 3, 1913.

The process of passing legislation went through a long, laborious process, which is my point in describing the process to you. 435 House Representatives, 100 Senators, and 1 President—a total of 536 individuals were involved in the passing of this bill, which included going through subcommittees a couple of times. These 535 state-residing individuals of Congress resided in states outside of Washington, D.C., and they represented the interests of their home states. They understood the Constitution protected its state citizens in that the National Government could not pass a direct tax on the people of their state. The bill before them was a fund-raising effort as a tax on the National Government itself.

Overall, the 535 state-residing Congress members who voted on the 16th Amendment did so with their own states' interests in mind. They would never have supported an amendment that imposed direct taxation on the citizens they represented and brought their state no value. Most importantly, the background of their anti-taxation stance, rooted in both historical precedent and political reality, played a decisive role in the passage of the 16th Amendment.

## The Background of American Taxation Prior to 1913

This country, the United States of America, was founded on the very basis of a tax rebellion. The 13 original colonies united against the taxation policies of England, a government that levied taxes on them without representation. The American Revolution was not just about independence; it was about financial freedom from an oppressive system where tax revenues flowed to a distant monarchy rather than benefiting the people who paid them. The inspiration from tax slavery is why the founding fathers put protection in place in the 1789 Constitution against a direct tax being imposed by the newly founded National Government on state citizens.

The first English settlers arrived in North America in the early 1600s, establishing colonies along the East Coast. Over the next two centuries, these colonies developed their own systems of governance, operating independently under charters granted by the British Crown. However, despite this self-governance, they remained economically tied to England, which imposed taxes to control trade and generate revenue.

Tensions erupted when Britain, facing debt from the Seven Years' War (1756–1763), sought to recover funds by taxing the colonies directly. The Stamp Act of 1765 and the Townshend Acts of 1767 forced colonists to pay taxes on paper goods, tea, and other imports. This taxation, imposed without colonial representation in Parliament, became a rallying cry— "No taxation without representation." It was this economic exploitation that united the colonies, leading to the Boston Tea Party in 1773, the Declaration of Independence in 1776, and ultimately, the formation of the United States of America, a nation that rejected unfair taxation.

Now, compare that historical struggle to modern taxation. When Americans pay income tax to the IRS, that money does not stay within their local city, county, or state; it goes to a third party acting as a federal governmental agency, much like how colonial tax revenues were funneled to England. The same principles that fueled the revolution remain relevant today. Understanding this connection is crucial, as the history of taxation in America did not end in 1776; it evolved into what we see today. As a side note, behind closed doors in England during the Revolutionary War of 1775 and the Federal

Reserve Act of 1913, the same banking families were and still are the ones printing the money and collecting usury fees (interest/taxes). Those with the power to tax are always the beneficiaries, and that is who the Federal Reserve is... they are the beneficiaries of private founding families collecting a tax, and most do not understand where much of the money goes.

When the 13 original colonies united against England, their goal was independence, not the creation of a centralized federal government with power over them. Each colony—Virginia, Delaware, Pennsylvania, Georgia, New Jersey, Connecticut, Massachusetts, South Carolina, New Hampshire, Maryland, New York, Rhode Island, and North Carolina— functioned as a self-governing entity with its own laws, economy, and leadership. These colonies did not view themselves as subdivisions of a larger nation, but as independent states cooperating in the fight for freedom.

Immediately after the United States was formed, the authority of governance remained at the state level. The Articles of Confederation (1781–1789) reflected this mindset, establishing a weak federal structure that left most power to the states. It wasn't until the revised Constitution was drafted in 1787 that a stronger federal government was proposed— but even then, it was limited in scope. The primary function of the National Government was to protect the colonies, which became states, from war with other countries. These were the only functions of creating a national government:

- Declare war
- Print paper money and mint coinage
- Issue regulations to control foreign trade and the trade carried out between the states.

- Run a postal service
- Control the granting of patents

Notice that none of these functions include being involved in local government within the individual republic states. There has never been, even as of today, by a vote of Congress, a plan put into place to create a government that meddled in the affairs of its state governing authority. This means it is the voluntary payments of American "taxpayers," most of whom have never owed the tax, that empower the national government's overreach. If you disagree with the pandemic, vaccines, 911, or other false flag operations, foreign affairs and wars, or a multitude of other things that even a non-conspiracy theorist can see, then stop funding the effort.

Prior to, during, and after the ratification of the Constitution, debate raged about the protection of individual rights. James Madison was a leading proponent of ensuring that American rights were explicitly stated in the Amendments to the Constitution, which are also called "the Bill of Rights," adequately named. To further emphasize the limited powers granted to the National Government by the Constitution, passing the final two of the ten original Amendments to the revised Constitution, also called The 9th and The 10th Amendments (1791), reinforced this principle by stating that powers not explicitly granted to the federal government were reserved for the states and the people. A summary of these two Amendments and the rights given thereof is expressed in a 1965 Supreme Court case opinion, Griswold v. State of Connecticut. Justice Arthur Goldberg states in summary of the 9th and 10th Amendments regarding individual protection against the National government:

*The Ninth Amendment, like its companion, the Tenth...was framed by James Madison and adopted by the States simply to make clear that the adoption of the Bill of Rights did not alter the plan that the Federal Government was to be a government of express and limited powers, and that all rights and powers not delegated to it were retained by the people and the individual States. Until today, no member of this Court has ever suggested that the Ninth Amendment meant anything else, and the idea that a federal court could ever use the Ninth Amendment to annul a law passed by the elected representatives of the people of the State of Connecticut would have caused James Madison no little wonder.*

## Washington, D.C., was created to be its own separate jurisdiction.

Washington, D.C., the federal seat of government, was formed in 1790 after the founding of the Country in 1775. It was designated as a 10-square-mile district as its distinct jurisdiction, separate from all the other Republic states. You may have to meditate on this distinction, which I will make for a while, because our brains, when we have heard terms our whole lives, have difficulty discerning differences, which is exceptionally important. The distinction is this – there exist two distinct, separate definitions of the phrase:

### United States

- The United States of America was created by the Constitution and is defined as a Constitutional Republic consisting of all 50 states of the Union. "We the People" represents the highest authority that our Constitution protects our rights, including our rights against a direct tax from our national government. (Article 1, Section 9, Clause 4)

- The UNITED STATES OF AMERICA was created by Congress and includes the District of Columbia and U.S. territories such as Guam, Puerto Rico, and the US Virgin Islands. The "State" (as in "Several States" coined by the 16th Amendment) is the highest authority and is statutory in nature by the exercise of its jurisdiction.

The IRS only has jurisdiction within the statutory UNITED STATES OF AMERICA and the subject therein. The term "U.S. Citizen" was created to be defined as a legislative person residing within Washington, D.C. You do not want to admit or be labeled as a "U.S. Citizen." If you ever read of a tax-related court case, pay close attention to the term U.S. Citizen as the ruling against the person is simply because they were subject to the tax ignorantly, and any of their tax protesting arguments do not fly when you admittedly, through opting into the tax system, have subjected yourself to their jurisdiction. You must opt out of that contract before you make any tax-protesting arguments. Better yet, once you opt out, there is nothing to argue about! Jurisdiction prohibits the IRS from coming against you... This, right here, is the basis of the unincorporated nonprofit association, an entity for which the IRS lacks jurisdiction.

This original constitutional structure was deliberately established to prevent outside taxation by a national government. The first governing document of the new nation, the Articles of Confederation (1777), enshrined the sovereign authority of each state to govern and tax its own people without interference. The National government could only request funds from the states, not demand them. The Articles also solidified the principle of state representation, with each state sending representatives to vote on national issues—a structure that continues in Congress today. It was later word trickery in redefining the name "UNITED STATES" that has led to so many not distinguishing between a tax that doesn't apply to them and ignorantly volunteering to pay it.

The Founding Fathers were relentless in ensuring this injustice would never be repeated. They explicitly prohibited the national government from directly taxing citizens. This protection was reinforced in the Constitution of 1789, which remains in effect today. It outlines the fundamental freedoms you are born with as an American—freedom of speech, freedom of religion, the right to bear arms, protection against unlawful searches and seizures, and the right to remain silent, among others. The right not to be levied a tax by a national government on you is one of these naturally born rights granted to us. Do you think there is a reason why we are not taught our Constitutional rights and taxation in school? If we were taught the truth, the IRS would cease to be involved in anybody's life except your military friends.

Because of the lack of knowledge of these critical rights, nobody knows they have built-in protection against federal taxation. Article 1, Section 9, Clause 4 of the Constitution is clear: the federal government cannot levy a direct tax on individuals. This raises an obvious question: If the Constitution protects you from federal taxation, how did the IRS gain the power to tax you?

This question leads to the deceptive mechanism that entangles Americans in a voluntary contractual relationship with the IRS. Millions unknowingly waive their constitutional protection each year by signing a 1040 IRS form—a legal contract that places them under federal tax jurisdiction, the District of Columbia, a/k/a "THE UNITED STATES" (all CAPS). The signature on this document creates a binding agreement, enforceable under penalty of perjury. It's not the tax that creates the obligation—it's the signed contract admitting liability and residency inside the District of Columbia.

The good news? There is a way to break this contract. We help people understand that they can reclaim their constitutional rights through a lawful process known as the Revocation of Election—a notarized affidavit sent to the IRS, formally ending the voluntary agreement. For self-employed individuals, forming an unincorporated nonprofit association (UNA) provides operational authority in commerce outside of the District of Columbia. A UNA is unincorporated and has no filing obligations with the IRS or Washington, D.C., ensuring that no contractual relationship is established from the start.

These are the lawful, constitutional steps to restore financial independence and eliminate the need to contract with the IRS. In chapter six, we will break down the IRS's contractual and administrative functional basis and how knowing how the system works eliminates fear.

## The Congressional Perspective of 1913

In 1913, members of Congress reflected on the foundational principles that shaped the American government, particularly regarding taxation, state sovereignty, and federal jurisdiction. Their discussions often returned to key historical events that established these principles, which would not allow them to knowingly pass a direct tax onto the citizens of their respective states:

- *The Revolutionary War (1775–1783)* was a direct revolt against forced taxation. Colonists rebelled against unjust

British taxes, which funded the Crown without benefiting the people paying them. This war was not just about independence—it was about securing economic freedom and eliminating external taxation without representation.

- *The Articles of Confederation (1777)* affirmed the sovereignty of each colony, which became a state of the new Country. Under this first Constitution, states governed independently and maintained complete control over their taxation, laws, and internal affairs. The National Government had no authority to impose taxes, relying instead on voluntary contributions from the states.

- *The revised Constitution of 1789* reassured the prohibition of federal taxation on state citizens. This protection is clearly outlined in Article 1, Section 9, Clause 4, which explicitly forbids direct taxation by the federal government. This clause was a direct safeguard against the very oppression the colonies had fought to escape.

- *The creation of Washington, D.C. in 1790* defined the federal government's jurisdiction. Unlike the 50 sovereign states, Washington, D.C. was established as a separate federal district, covering only ten square miles. This distinction meant that the federal government's direct authority was limited to that jurisdiction, preventing it from overstepping into state affairs.

Congress, when convening in Washington, D.C., legislates only for the federal government. The laws created in this district apply specifically to federal entities, agencies, and employees. While Congress oversees national policies, its authority over taxation and governance was never meant to supersede the sovereignty of individual states. It is estimated that of all laws passed by Congress, 85% of them apply only to this limited jurisdiction and not to the Constitutional Republic states. But here is an important key to knowing which laws that are passed do apply!!!

The laws that do apply to the Constitutional Republic must be published in the National Register. If any law applies outside the District of Columbia, it is required by the Federal Register Act to be an implementing regulation and published in the Federal Register to give notice to the American people.

Michael L. White, Federal Attorney in the Office of the Federal Register (National Archives), has stated that:

*"Our records indicate that the Internal Revenue Service has not promulgated (published) in the Federal Register a requirement to make an income tax return."*

As such, the Federal Income Tax is only applicable within the District of Columbia and validated by the Legislative Intent of the 16th Amendment. Thus, there is no imposed duty for Americans to file any income tax return.

Viewing these foundational facts, it is easy to see the vantage point of the Congressmen by which the 16th Amendment bill was presented to them. This also leads to the question that cannot be avoided: How could the 16th Amendment be passed as an amendment to the Constitution while contradicting the very Constitution? In other words, Article 1, Section 9, Clause 4 of the 1789 Constitution states that the Federal government cannot lay a direct tax on a State citizen, so how could the 16th Amendment tax State citizens?

The answer lies in the precise way the 16th Amendment was framed and applied. Congress could not pass an amendment that directly violated the Constitution—if it had, the amendment would have been deemed unconstitutional and invalid from the outset. Instead, the 16th Amendment was carefully constructed not to override Article 1, Section 9, Clause 4, but to introduce a tax **OUTSIDE OF** the existing constitutional framework.

The 16th Amendment does not contradict Article 1, Section 9, Clause 4 of the 1789 Constitution. The 16th Amendment was levied as a tax on the National Government and does not apply to anybody living in the Republic States who is not a Federal employee. It only applies to residents of Washington, D.C., and Federal government employees because this is the statutory UNITED STATES (all CAPS) created by Congress.

In concluding this subsection on the 16th Amendment, it is essential to examine the legislative intent behind the law. Every law begins as an idea, and in the case of the 16th Amendment, there is documented evidence from its earliest stages. The Congressional record from 1909, when the amendment was first proposed, provides critical insight into the true purpose behind its creation. The Congressional records are the meeting minutes that dictate what occurred in the congressional sessions.

A pivotal moment in this process was President William H. Taft's written address to the U.S. Senate, in which he formally introduced the 16th Amendment and made its legislative intent unmistakably clear. His address explicitly indicated that the amendment was designed only to authorize the government to impose taxes on its own employees, not on private citizens of the sovereign states.

Taft's unique legal expertise made his role in this matter even more significant. In 1921, he became the only U.S. President ever to serve as Chief Justice of the Supreme Court, cementing his status as a legal authority on constitutional interpretation. His appointment followed the tenure of Chief Justice E.B. White, who had previously dissented in the landmark 1895 case Pollock v. Farmers' Loan & Trust Company, where the Supreme Court struck down the federal income tax as unconstitutional. Unlike White, who sought to legalize direct taxation, Taft's own actions and statements suggested alignment with the idea that taxation should be limited in scope.

No other U.S. President has ever held both the highest executive and judicial offices, nor had a deeper legal understanding of the 16th Amendment's implications than William H. Taft. His direct involvement in its introduction provides undeniable clarity regarding the amendment's original intent—an intent that has been largely misunderstood and misrepresented over time.

## Congressional Record - Senate - June 16, 1909

Taft's address to the Senate and House of Representatives explicitly acknowledged the constitutional limitations imposed by the Supreme Court's ruling in Pollock v. Farmers' Loan & Trust Company. Recognizing that the federal government lacked the power to impose a direct income tax on the Constitutional Republic State Citizens, Taft advocated for the National Government itself.

[From Pages 3344 – 3345] The Secretary read as follows: To the Senate and House of Representatives:

*It is the constitutional duty of the President, from time to time, to recommend such measures to Congress as he shall judge necessary and expedient. In my inaugural address, immediately preceding this present extraordinary session of Congress, I invited attention to the necessity for a revision of the tariff at this session and stated the principles upon which I thought the revision should be affected. I referred to the then rapidly increasing deficit and pointed out the obligation on the part of the framers of the tariff bill to arrange the duty so as to secure an adequate income, and suggested that if it was not possible to do so by import duties, new kinds of taxation must be adopted, and among them, I recommended a graduated inheritance tax as correct in principle and as certain and easy of collection.*

The House of Representatives has adopted the suggestion and has provided it in the bill it passed for the collection of such a tax. In the Senate, the action of its Finance Committee and the course of the debate indicate that it may not agree to this provision, and it is now proposed to make up the deficit by the imposition of a general income tax, in form and substance of almost exactly the same character as, that which in the case of *Pollock v. Farmer's Loan* and Trust Company (157 U.S., 429) was held by the Supreme Court to be a direct tax, and therefore not within the power of the Federal Government to Impose unless apportioned among the several States according to population. This new proposal, which I did not discuss in my inaugural address or in my message at the opening of the present session, makes it appropriate for me to submit to Congress certain additional recommendations.

Again, it is clear that by the enactment of the proposed law, Congress will not be bringing money into the Treasury to meet the present deficiency. The decision of the Supreme Court in the income-tax cases deprived the National Government of a power which, by reason of previous decisions of the court, it was generally supposed that the government had. It is undoubtedly a power the National Government ought to have. It might be indispensable to the Nation's life in great crises. Although I have not considered a constitutional amendment as necessary to exercise certain phases of this power, a mature consideration has satisfied me that an amendment is the only proper course for its establishment to its full extent.

I therefore recommend to Congress that both Houses, by a two-thirds vote, shall propose an amendment to the Constitution conferring the power to levy an income tax upon the National Government without apportionment among the States in proportion to population.

Four years after President Taft championed this bill, the 16th Amendment was ratified in 1913. Its passage was not a rushed or haphazard decision but the result of careful legal and political maneuvering to ensure it would pass through Congress. The amendment was designed to address the constitutional limitations outlined in Pollock v. Farmers' Loan & Trust Company, ensuring that the federal government could NOT collect income tax without requiring apportionment among the states. So, the crucial detail that is often overlooked is that this tax was intended to be levied on the National/Federal government itself as a means of generating revenue—not as a direct tax on private citizens residing in the sovereign states.

The legislative process leading up to the ratification makes this clear. The 535 congressional representatives (435 members of the House and 100 Senators) who voted on the amendment did so with full awareness of its scope and impact. No representative would have approved a measure that imposed a direct tax on their constituents, as doing so would have been politically damaging and unconstitutional. Instead, their votes reflected an understanding that the amendment provided the federal government with a structured mechanism to generate funds without infringing on the rights of state citizens who were not federal employees or residing in federal jurisdictions.

This fundraising effort of a federal income tax to be levied on the National Government was the selling point to Congress. Something much more sinister was in the actual works behind the scenes, though. If you are not a "conspiracy theorist," then brace yourself to carefully analyze the next chapter and how the agenda would be unfolded after the passing of the $16^{th}$ Amendment.

# *Chapter Five: The Agenda Of Taxation Is "National Debt"*

So, how did this happen? How did the American people accept an income tax system that was never lawfully applied to them and yet became a part of everyday life? More importantly, how does one step outside of it?

So, to address the question of how many people have begun paying the federal income tax over time, we must highlight the agenda. Without seeing the agenda, it is impossible to connect the dots. In the early days after 1913, it was the propaganda machine firing up the press, fueling the advertisement of the debt machine in their own terms, that made the truth of the banker's plan too great for the highly deceived American public, with access to no information-sharing tools to figure out. Remember, when this plan took root in 1913, there was no internet, cell phone, or fax machine for people to communicate. There was no social media, YouTube videos, or alternative media to highlight the fraud that was being perpetrated. It was the morning newspapers, controlled by the bankers, who controlled the narrative by means of possessing all the money, painting the picture through published news stories that our nation was incurring a national debt, which placed a false ownership on good-hearted Americans who began to believe they must opt into the tax system to pay it down, allegedly. Paying down the "national debt" is a feat that can never be accomplished because it represents the continual creation of money from nothing through loans with compounding interest.

Take a close look at the dates below—two independent laws signed into effect by President Woodrow Wilson:

- February 3, 1913 – The 16th Amendment
- December 23, 1913 – The Federal Reserve Act

At first glance, they might seem unrelated. Many people don't see the connection—some have never even thought about it. In my conversations, I often ask: Did you know the 16th Amendment gives the IRS the authority to collect taxes? Most people don't. And when I ask what the Federal Reserve actually does, who controls it, and how it came into existence, the response is often the same—uncertainty.

As discussed in the last chapter, on February 3, 1913, the 16th Amendment was ratified, giving Congress the power to levy a federal income tax—something the Supreme Court had just previously ruled unconstitutional in Pollock v. Farmers' Loan & Trust Co. (1895). This is why this particular federal income tax, in becoming an Amendment to the Constitution, did not apply to state citizens as prior failed attempts did. It was well understood that a proposed direct tax on Americans would never be approved. The trick was to propose a tax to be an Amendment to the Constitution without contradicting the Constitution, as attempts in the past did. That's why it was voted on virtually unanimously by Congress, as it was not a tax on individual

State citizens but rather the "federal" government itself. That's why it is called a "federal" income tax – a tax on the federal government.

Working harmoniously with the efforts of passing the 16th Amendment, as part of a patiently planned out agenda, without the Congressmen's foreknowledge who were presented the bill, just ten months later, on December 23, 1913, President Wilson signed the Federal Reserve Act into law, creating the Federal Reserve System—a private banking cartel that has controlled the U.S. money supply ever since. The Federal Reserve Act established a central banking system with the authority to print money, manipulate interest rates, and loan funds to the government, all while remaining privately controlled. This new system allowed the government to operate on deficit spending, borrowing money rather than being limited by tangible assets.

What cannot be overemphasized is that these hijackers of our currency, under the guise of the "Federal Reserve," charge our U.S. Treasury interest for the money "loaned," which is printed from thin air. It's an imaginary, engineered economic phenomenon called "the National Debt." After all, what product can you think of besides sunshine, rain, sleet, or snow that can be created from nothing?

The "national debt" is money created from nothing and "loaned" to our

U.S. Treasury. The U.S. Treasury, which our Constitution states in Article 1, section 8, clause two, that Congress shall have power to coin money... but in 1913, via the Federal Reserve Act, that power to coin money was given to a private organization labeled "Federal Reserve". So, ironically, while the 16th Amendment was carefully crafted not to contradict the Constitution, it was the Federal Reserve Act that was unconstitutional by replacing our authority to coin money with "Federal Reserve Notes" issued into existence by an outside private 3rd party. For those who may never have stopped and analyzed the dollar bills in your pocket right now, the end of this chapter will show you some things. The word "note" for "Federal Reserve Note," printed at the top, means it's a debt instrument and not something of value. In other words, if you have a $20 bill, a $10 bill, and three $1 bills in your pocket, it represents that you actually are negative $33 and not positive $33. Meditate on this for a while! Only because of widespread faith in these funny-looking bills, for the time being, until the Ponzi scheme collapses, is what allows you to buy something with those "notes."

So, what ties the 16th Amendment and the Federal Reserve Act laws together? The connection is actually the IRS! The IRS, or Internal Revenue Service, was created to collect tax revenue from the 16th Amendment. The IRS, which was created in 1913, along with these two acts of law, is a funding mechanism for the federal government. However, its primary function has become a collection arm of the Federal Reserve to collect interest on the "national debt." So, once the laws were in place, a money-creating and lending machine of the Federal Reserve, with private people behind the mechanism, began, and the 16th Amendment created the IRS to collect taxes, which, in turn, much of that money pays the interest on the money created from nothing.

All that was missing was selling an agenda to the American people. The agenda began a never-ending drumbeat marketing effort, which we still hear the sound of the drums today, in that our Country is incurring a national debt, and good taxpayers need to contribute. The IRS has continually rewarded the masked men behind the Federal Reserve since 1913 by paying usury fees for the money that created nothing. Just in case you haven't connected the dots in this paragraph, the Federal Reserve has given no value to our Country but, in return, receives continual "taxpayer money" for the privilege of waving a magic wand and "poof, here's more money we are giving to your US Government."

Understanding how these two pivotal laws—one passed in February 1913, the other in December 1913—transformed America's financial structure is key to seeing the bigger picture. This chapter is designed to unravel how the events of that year birthed the modern national debt, created its collection agency, the IRS, and set in motion an economic structure that has placed America under the thumb of central banking ever since. It's brought our Country to its knees in every aspect and will one day soon pull the magic carpet out from underneath our feet.

Let's start with the dates. The 16th Amendment was ratified on February 3, 1913, officially granting Congress the power to impose a federal income tax. Just ten months later, on December 23, 1913, while many members of Congress were on holiday break, the Federal Reserve Act was signed into law. The timing of these events was far from accidental. Understanding what happened in 1913 is crucial to grasping how the U.S. financial system was fundamentally reshaped—creating a structure that most Americans unknowingly fund to this day.

I have a question for you—a question designed to drive a significant point home. Pretend you were alive in 1913 and resided in one of the 48 states of our Republic (Alaska & Hawaii were not states yet). Do you know what would have happened to your economic situation—your income, your family's finances, and your neighbors' livelihoods—on February 3, 1913, when the 16th Amendment was passed, approving a federal income tax?

The answer is nothing. Absolutely nothing changed for anyone residing in any of the Republic states. In fact, it was widely understood at the time that the 16th Amendment did not apply to the average American citizen. It was explicitly intended for those who lived in Washington, D.C. or worked directly for the federal government. The notion that every working American would automatically be subject to federal income tax was simply not part of the law's original scope. It took a while for the plan to entirely result in voluntary servitude, and the next date was the final cornerstone.

The events of December 23, 1913, reshaped the world's financial landscape in ways most people fail to grasp. This was not just a policy shift—it was a conspiracy that fundamentally altered the course of banking, money, taxation, and the economic system as a whole. Many avoid using the word "conspiracy" to maintain credibility, but to discuss the Federal Reserve without acknowledging the deception behind its creation would be dishonest. The reality is unavoidable—like the elephant in the room that people would rather not recognize, so they aren't labeled as a tin foil hat-wearing unicorn telling everybody that the sky is falling.

Volumes have been written about the Federal Reserve Act and its implications, and some of the most brilliant minds have exposed the hidden agenda behind its passage. For a deeper exploration of the secret meeting that took place in 1910 on Jekyll Island, Georgia—where a small group of private bankers and Senator Nelson Aldrich orchestrated a plan to seize control of the U.S. money supply—I highly recommend The Creature from Jekyll Island by G. Edward Griffin.

To simplify what happened, let's use the game of Monopoly as an analogy. Imagine four players sitting down to play, each receiving $1,500 in Monopoly money. The game begins fairly—each player rolls the dice, buys property, collects rent, and follows the established rules. The bank operates independently, distributing money based on the game's mechanics without favoring any player. In this scenario, the bank is neutral, much like the U.S. economy before 1913.

Now imagine that, in the middle of the game, an uninvited fifth player suddenly takes a seat at the table and declares himself the new bank. Without contributing anything, he seizes control of the money supply and begins charging interest on every dollar in circulation—including the money players already have. Naturally, the other players protest: "That's not fair! You weren't even part of the game to begin with!"

This is indeed what happened to the U.S. economy in 1913. During the holiday season, while much of Congress was away, a deceptive bill was quietly pushed through, handing control of the nation's currency to private bankers under the guise of the "Federal Reserve." Public outcry followed, particularly in the first few decades after its passage, as those who lived through the transition recognized the blatant theft that had occurred. Even President Woodrow Wilson—who played a role in its passage—later expressed deep regret over what had transpired. Read in this image below his words of regret:

Woodrow Wilson after signing the Federal Reserve Act of 1913

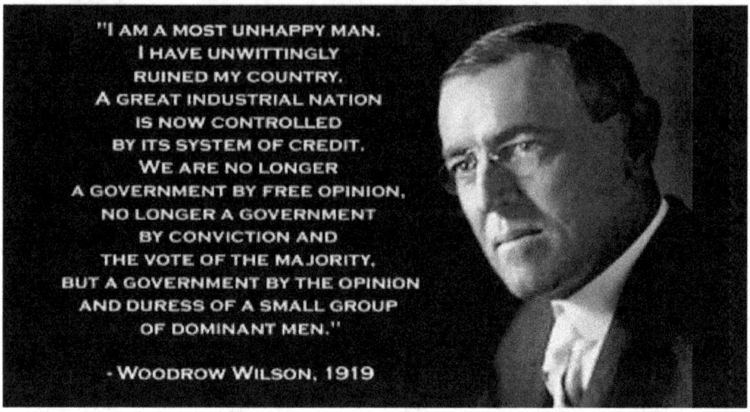


Like the Monopoly analogy, an independent group of powerful banking families—including the Rothschilds, Rockefellers, and J.P. Morgan— took control of America's money supply. In turn, after creating money from nothing, they loaned this money back to the government, with interest. This is the foundation of what they call the National Debt.

Think about the absurdity of this system: If an ordinary citizen writes a check from a bank account that doesn't exist, they go to jail. But the Federal Reserve was created to do just that—print money from nothing on a bank account that never existed and lend it to the U.S. Treasury, making it legal through legislation. They effectively control every dollar in circulation, manipulating the economy while ensuring they always remain the ultimate beneficiaries. In simplest terms, they made it "law" that a few private families could steal from all of us by virtue of collecting interest on their "loans".

Understanding this system is crucial when examining the role of the IRS. The connection between the Federal Reserve and taxation is deliberate— one fuels the other. And if you've ever questioned the concept of inflation, you've just found your answer. Inflation is not some natural economic force; it is the direct result of the Federal Reserve printing money out of thin air.

Even as a child, I found the idea of inflation perplexing. I remember hearing that a bottle of Coca-Cola cost just five cents in the 1940s. By the 1980s, that same bottle was fifty cents. The steady erosion of the dollar's purchasing power was framed as an inevitable part of economic progress, but the truth is far more calculated. Inflation is not merely rising prices— it is the result of an expanding money supply that dilutes the value of each dollar. Over time, this shift ensures that the real wealth—the purchasing power of money—flows away from the people and into the hands of those who control its issuance. The Federal Reserve did not just hijack the banking system in 1913; it rewrote the rules of the game entirely.

The major component of the tax scheme that hasn't been addressed in this chapter—when discussing the 16th Amendment and taxation—is the oldest ambition of those seeking power: controlling a nation's or kingdom's currency and taxing its people. Jesus Himself addressed this principle, stating in Matthew 17:25-26 that "the kings of the earth" tax strangers, not their own families. Taxation has always been a tool of control used by those in power to extract wealth from those they govern.

America's founding fathers and true patriots were always on guard against banking interests attempting to seize control of the nation's currency. A central bank holds absolute authority over a country's banking system and money supply. The explanation of the danger of a central bank is that one bank, or financial head, controls all monetary decisions for all banks under its control. The Federal Reserve is exactly that—a privately controlled institution that dictates national banking policies, as any bank wanting to do business in this Country must be connected to the Federal Reserve system and its money supply.

The conspiracy of 1913 to establish the Federal Reserve was the third attempt at a banking takeover. The first two failed:

1. The First Bank of the United States (1791-1811) was established by Alexander Hamilton. This central bank faced opposition from Thomas Jefferson and James Madison, who viewed it as a threat to state sovereignty and individual liberty. Its charter expired in 1811 due to public resistance.

2. The Second Bank of the United States (1815-1835). A second attempt followed, but President Andrew Jackson fiercely opposed it, calling its leadership a "den of vipers and thieves." He blocked its charter renewal in 1836, dismantling what he saw as an unconstitutional financial monopoly.

The bankers didn't give up in trying to establish a Central bank which they would control. In 1913, they finally succeeded—this time using secrecy and political maneuvering to establish the Federal Reserve. Unlike before, this central bank was disguised as a solution to economic instability and passed into law when much of Congress was away for the holidays. The bigger picture of the agenda was contingent on passing a taxation law through Congress first, no matter how the bill's legislative intent was spelled out, so later, when they hijacked the currency, they could get paid, and paid, and paid, and paid... by manipulating the intent of that tax law. Without the taxation law coming first, it would be too obvious that the bankers would be the beneficiaries of a tax had the Federal Reserve been formed first.

A symbolic detail reflects how the Federal Reserve honors its origins— Alexander Hamilton, the man behind the first central bank, is enshrined on the $10 bill. While many recognize him as the first

Secretary of the Treasury, his true legacy—at least in the eyes of banking elites—is setting the foundation for financial control over the nation.

How else would Alexander Hamilton secure a prestigious place in history, carried in the wallets of every American? His presence on the $10 bill is no accident; it's a tribute from the banking elite to the man who paved the way for centralized financial control.

Take a closer look at U.S. currency. Each bill bears two seals—on the left, the Federal Reserve seal (representing the banking cartel), and on the right, the U.S. Treasury seal (representing the American people). Now, notice a pattern: George Washington, Thomas Jefferson, Abraham Lincoln, Andrew Jackson, Ulysses S. Grant, and Benjamin Franklin—all men who fought for the nation's sovereignty, real American patriots—face right toward the U.S. Treasury seal.

Alexander Hamilton? The sole exception. He faces left, directly toward the Federal Reserve seal.

A mere coincidence? Or a silent acknowledgment of where his true allegiance always lay, and a way the bankers put it right in our face that they are the traitors?

To make it clear where Alexander Hamilton's true allegiance lay, the $10 bill includes a revealing detail. Unlike any other U.S. bill, it features the words "We The People" printed in red—yet Hamilton has his back turned to them. No other bill is written in red letters, "We The People".

This isn't just a design choice. Every other historical figure on U.S. currency faces toward the U.S. Treasury seal, representing the American people. Hamilton alone faces left, toward the Federal Reserve seal—the very institution that thrives on the central banking model he introduced.

The phrase "We the People" stands for self-governance, the foundation of American democracy. Its placement of "We the People" on the $10 bill, alongside Hamilton's deliberate positioning of his head/back turned the other way, is a quiet reminder that his legacy wasn't about empowering the people; it was about empowering the banks and selling out the people. They clearly show us on the $10 bill that Hamilton was a traitor, as they themselves are traitors to our Country. In 1913, the monetary control system over the people he fought for was fully realized with the passing of the Federal Reserve Act—the ultimate consolidation of financial power.

How is it that so many Americans voluntarily pay a tax they don't legally owe? To understand this, let's chronologically lay out the agenda.

On February 3, 1913, the 16th Amendment was quietly passed, with the public at large feeling no impact on the tax that was passed into law, allegedly giving Congress the power to levy an income tax. However, its actual legal impact was limited, as discussed many times already; it applied only to those under federal jurisdiction, such as government employees and residents of Washington, D.C. If you worked for the military or another federal agency, you likely learned of the new tax quickly and had no choice but to comply. For the rest of the country, it largely went unnoticed.

Unlike today, there was no internet, no independent news sources, and no way for the average citizen to investigate new laws. The only source of information was the morning newspaper, which was easy to control. With no widespread awareness, the public remained uninformed about the true nature of the income tax.

Beginning in 1914, another narrative was being carefully introduced: the idea of a "national debt." This so-called debt was nothing more than the Federal Reserve's scheme of printing money from nothing and lending it to the U.S. Treasury—at interest. These loans didn't just happen once; they became a continuous cycle, ensuring that the debt could never be repaid. In fact, the system depends on the debt growing indefinitely, because without new loans, the money supply itself would collapse.

This is the reality of the system put in place in 1913—a system designed not to serve the people but to permanently bind them to the debt of an economy controlled by the magicians granted the power to create money from nothing, the private bankers.

After 1913, with the concept of a "national debt" beginning to be planted in the public's mind, many Americans assumed it was their duty to help pay it off. The message was clear: A good citizen contributes to reducing the debt, and therefore, those who do not pay their taxes are not good citizens. I can imagine in my mind how there had to have been sharp divisions in the households and in the streets between the deceived "righteous" agreeing to pay the tax and those resisting a tax they had never paid.

Imagine living in South Carolina in the early 20th century. For years, you've read about this ever-growing national debt in the newspapers. Wanting to do your part, you tell your wife you're going to file, submit, and sign a tax contract with the IRS—believing it's the right thing to do for the country. Over time, this idea became ingrained in American life.

By the next generation, paying the IRS was simply a given. Young workers entering the job market had automatic deductions from their paychecks. When tax season arrived, they voluntarily signed the contract—unaware that by doing so, they were agreeing to be taxpayers. And just like that, the system took hold.

The good news? Well, the "national debt" is imaginary. You don't have to continually sign contracts agreeing to a tax you do not owe. There are ways out of this scheme, methods that have been discussed earlier. The first step is understanding how it all began.

**Disclaimer:** This work is intended to provide a reader-friendly overview of significant historical events, Congressional acts, laws, and quotations. To enhance clarity and accessibility, some details have been intentionally omitted or condensed. Readers interested in a comprehensive understanding of these topics are encouraged to consult additional sources.

# *Chapter Six: Knowledge Eliminates Fear Of The Tax System*

As a young boy, my mother would tuck me into bed each night in our medium-sized house. After she had turned off the lights, I would see a shadowy figure cast on the wall at the foot of my bed. My imagination turned that shadow into a menacing presence, something to be feared. I remember pulling the covers over my head, hoping it would be gone if I looked again.

For what felt like an eternity in my childhood mind, I was afraid of that figure on the wall—until the day I finally decided to analyze it. Night after night, I watched how it shifted and changed until I figured it out: it was simply the moonlight casting a shadow from the large tree in our backyard. Some nights, the shadow moved slightly with the wind, and on nights with no moon, it disappeared entirely.

The IRS is much like that shadowy figure on my bedroom wall—

a fear that exists only because of misunderstanding. For many, the mere thought of not paying taxes or receiving a letter from the IRS casts a dark shadow over their psyche.

The agency is perceived as a looming, all-powerful force capable of devastating lives with the stroke of a pen. Any interaction with the IRS feels like staring at a monstrous silhouette, one that might reach out and strike at any moment.

This fear runs so deep that people will do anything to avoid confrontation, including voluntarily filing tax contracts and handing over their money year after year, despite the fact that the tax may not even apply to them. Most Americans never question whether they are legally required to pay, simply assuming that participation is mandatory. After all, everyone else does it, and the consequences of resisting seem far too terrifying even to consider.

But what if the IRS, this shadowy monster on the wall, was nothing more than an illusion? What if the fear exists only because most Americans don't understand how federal income tax law, IRS procedures, and jurisdiction actually work?

The truth is that the 16th Amendment, ratified in 1913, did not create an unlimited taxing authority. Instead, it established a specific and limited tax structure, one that applies only under particular conditions. The IRS does not operate as a law enforcement agency with unchecked power over every citizen. Rather, it functions as a systematic accounting and administrative body that gains jurisdiction through voluntary submission when individuals unknowingly enter into tax contracts.

This is where the most significant deception lies: implied consent. Americans are led to believe they are legally obligated to file a return and pay income taxes, but in reality, jurisdiction is established only when a person voluntarily steps into the system, usually without even realizing it. The IRS does not come knocking on doors demanding participation; instead, it invites individuals into the tax system through procedural mechanisms cleverly disguised as legal obligations.

The entire operation thrives on fear and ignorance. However, once you recognize the limited reach of the federal income tax system, how jurisdiction is acquired, and how the IRS operates through automated enforcement rather than omnipotent authority, the fear dissolves. Like that childhood shadow, it was never a real threat. It was only a trick of perception all along—a carefully crafted illusion designed to keep people compliant.

The only way to break free from this illusion is through knowledge. Because the IRS, much like that childhood shadow, only has power if you let it.

It's essential to address the personification of the IRS right away because this misconception fuels unnecessary fear. In daily conversations, I've noticed that people unconsciously assign human qualities to the IRS, as if it were a living, breathing entity with personal vendettas. Society has conditioned us to see the IRS as a relentless school bully, waiting by the lockers to ambush us, punch us in the face, and snatch our lunch money the moment we make a wrong move.

I recall a time when I was teaching a group about how the system really works. One individual, overwhelmed with concern, kept asking fear-based questions that all shared the same underlying assumption: that the IRS was actively hunting him down. At one point, I looked at him and joked, "From the way you're asking these questions, I imagine that when you drive home, you're constantly checking your rearview mirror—like the IRS is tailing you in an unmarked van."

The room broke out in laughter, but the point was clear: the IRS is not an omnipresent force lurking in the shadows, watching your every move. The agency is not following you home, tracking your phone, or sitting outside your house in a surveillance van. In reality, the IRS doesn't have to care about you at all because the system runs on automation, not human oversight.

Here's the truth: The IRS does not "come after" people—it waits for people to come to it.

There are no IRS agents monitoring your bank transactions in real time. There are no government officials scanning security cameras to see where you shop. There are no teams of investigators digging into your personal life unless you invite them to do so. The entire system is structured around voluntary submission. The IRS only gains jurisdiction when you enter into a tax contract by signing, filing, and effectively agreeing that you owe a tax.

Once that contract is signed, everything is automated:

1. If you miss a deadline, a computer-generated letter is automatically mailed to you. The letter is mailed because a) you entered into a contract with them in the past and have not revoked it, and b) you received money reported in your social security number in the year you missed a deadline. This is an automated letter.

2. If you fail to respond, the system escalates the enforcement process—again, without human intervention. The system gives you thirty days to respond, and with no response, they go to a system of more administrative letters. They count non-responses as your consent to their request in the letter.

3. If the system determines a liability exists (because you voluntarily acknowledged it by not responding to their sequence of letters), the case is eventually assigned to an internal debt collector, not some shadowy IRS agent personally hunting you down.

No human IRS employee is personally invested in your case. It is a mindless and impersonal systematic administrative accounting system. No matter how important a person thinks they are, nobody is targeted intentionally. If you place yourself liable to the IRS through entering into contracts and receiving money to your social security number, then you may receive a letter requesting unfiled tax contracts to be filed. It is always the filing of the yearly tax contract that you sign that creates the tax liability, and not the tax law itself, unless you are a federal employee. They must get your agreement by your signature on a contract or by you not responding to their sequence of several administrative letters.

Before I dive deeper into the actual mechanisms of tax contracts, accounting, and the administrative process, it's essential first to break down the most common misconceptions—especially the deeply ingrained belief that the IRS is some all-powerful schoolyard bully waiting to take your lunch. Because once you see the IRS for what it really is—an impersonal, automated financial system that depends entirely on your compliance, the fear begins to lose its grip.

This is a common first reaction when people are confronted with the idea that they might not actually be required to pay a "federal" income tax— they immediately assume that prison awaits anyone who even entertains the thought. But where does this perception come from? Fear. The deeply ingrained fear that the IRS is an unstoppable force, ready to punish anyone who questions its authority.

If you read chapter 4, you'll remember that the 16th Amendment, the very law that grants the IRS its taxing authority, only applies to specific groups—those residing in Washington, D.C., corporate federal territories, and federal employees. It is called a "federal" income tax because it was designed to tax the federal government itself, not state citizens living in any of the fifty states. This distinction is not some obscure loophole—it is a fundamental limitation of federal taxation that has existed since 1913 and remains in place today.

In fact, the only reason the 16th Amendment could have been passed in 1913 was that it adhered to the constraints of the 1789 U.S. Constitution, which explicitly forbids the federal government from imposing a direct tax on state citizens without apportionment. If the 16th Amendment had attempted to tax state residents directly, it would have been unconstitutional from the outset. The same principle applies today—the federal government cannot enforce an income tax on you unless you voluntarily agree to it.

And that's exactly where tax contracts come into play. By signing and filing a tax return, you are legally agreeing to be treated as a federal taxpayer, bringing yourself under the IRS's jurisdiction by your own consent. This is the hidden mechanism by which millions of Americans unknowingly submit to a tax that was never meant to apply to them in the first place.

Our fast-food society has conditioned us to seek out so-called "experts" for advice on things we know little about. On the surface, this seems reasonable—why spend years learning about something when a professional can explain it in minutes? But here's the problem: The very systems we rely on—whether in law, finance, healthcare, fitness, religion, taxation, or the courts—are not designed around the truth. They are structured around licensing, training, and regulation, all operating within a framework that serves an ulterior motive.

And what are the two common denominators? Money and control.

If your goal is to find the truth, you might discover that the "experts"— the ones supposedly equipped to help—are often the last people who will lead you in the right direction.

Think about it:

- Have you ever sought justice in court? Chances are, you didn't get it.
- Have you ever needed legal help? A lawyer may have complicated your situation instead of resolving it.
- Have you ever trusted a doctor to heal you? Many will prescribe a pill or recommend surgery, treating symptoms without addressing the root problem.
- And if you wanted to understand who God is, would you really find the answers by walking into any of the thousands of religious institutions and asking to speak to the leader?

The uncomfortable truth is that many of the systems we trust aren't designed to serve us—they are designed to keep us dependent.

The principle of "trained, licensed professionals" applies nowhere more clearly than in the tax industry. Whether it's accountants, CPAs, tax attorneys, or enrolled agents, all of these professionals operate within a framework dictated by IRS statutes and codes. But here's the catch—ask any honest tax professional, and they'll admit that these statutes are ambiguous, subject to interpretation, and often contradictory. Yet, the more significant issue—the question of jurisdiction—remains ignored. Allow me to repeat this: jurisdiction is ignored. This means your tax professional is completely useless to you.

If the IRS lacks the legal authority to impose a federal income tax on individuals living in any of the 50 states, then it doesn't matter what their statutes say, because none of them apply.

But why would tax professionals ever question this? Their entire livelihood depends on people continuing to file tax contracts. If individuals stopped paying federal income taxes, these professionals would have no business. Their training—rooted in IRS statutes, licensing requirements, and a career-dependent belief in the system—ensures that they never explore the reality that most people never owe the tax in the first place. In fact, their role is essential in keeping the system running—not because they're inherently deceptive, but because they are products of a system designed to perpetuate itself.

Imagine this scenario: You decide to pursue a career in accounting. You earn your degree, pass your exams, and eventually become a Certified Public Accountant (CPA). Your study material? IRS statutes and codes. Your goal? It is to help individuals navigate the system by filing tax returns efficiently, and maybe even help them "save" money by reducing their tax burden.

But here's the irony: The entire foundation of the profession is built on a false premise. The issue isn't about how much tax someone owes—it's whether they owed anything at all in the first place. And in most cases, they didn't.

This isn't about bad people working in the tax industry—it's about good people unknowingly participating in a system designed to mislead. The deception isn't in the professionals themselves but in the framework that trained them. The IRS operates on a system of voluntary compliance, where individuals unknowingly contract themselves to taxation. Without your signature, there is no liability.

And yet, the system is sustained by an army of professionals whose financial stability depends on never questioning that simple fact. I suppose there is an implied thought that "this must all be true and correct if my job is based on the IRS, which propagates this very large industry."

The misperception about people going to jail for simply not paying taxes is almost comical to me. It stems from a lack of information and a failure to understand the circumstances behind each case.

For example, someone recently told me that Martha Stewart went to jail for not paying taxes. I had to correct them—she was actually convicted of insider trading, obstruction of justice, and lying to investigators. Her case had nothing to do with taxes.

Then there's Wesley Snipes. People often bring him up as an example of someone who went to prison for not paying taxes. And while it's true that he had tax-related legal issues. Do we ever stop to ask what exactly landed him in trouble? Context matters.

Wesley Snipes, like many others, realized that he wasn't actually liable for federal income tax in the way the IRS claimed. But here's where he went wrong—he didn't just remove himself from the system. Instead, he filed a tax return/contract demanding that the IRS refund him $7.5 million for taxes he had previously paid.

And here's the key point: Once you sign a tax contract and send money to the IRS, that money is gone. There's no undoing it. Or, as I often say, "You just donated money to your least favorite charity."

The mistake Snipes made was not understanding how jurisdiction works. Instead of stepping away, he actively challenged the system while still playing by its rules. The IRS wasn't punishing him for not paying taxes— they caught him "lying" on a signed tax contract. Since he had voluntarily filed returns for years, he had already legally affirmed that he owed the tax.

So, when he later claimed the IRS owed him millions, they used his own signed contracts against him in court to prove that he had, in fact, agreed to those payments year after year. That's what got him convicted—not simply refusing to pay.

Isn't it most important to understand what actually lands someone in jail? The fear of imprisonment is what fuels that "shadowy figure at the foot of your bed"—the same fear I alluded to in the introduction of this chapter. When we hear about people going to prison over taxes, our minds bring that monster to life.

But fear thrives on ignorance. The key to eliminating fear is understanding exactly what puts someone in harm's way. There's a reason why only a handful of people have been imprisoned over tax issues, and there's also a 100% foolproof way to ensure you never will.

Since the fear of going to jail is the primary motivation for paying taxes, let's look at both the statistics of people ending up in jail for a tax-related "crime" and then the formula for going to jail, so you know there really is nothing to be afraid of with knowledge.

## The Statistics of Landing in Jail

There are approximately 350 million Americans living in the fifty republic states. I am not sure how many of these people work for the federal government, but those would be the only ones required to file a tax return and pay taxes. My point is this: of the 350 million Americans, only 2,300 tax crimes were brought to court in 2023, and in roughly 2,200 of those cases, the individuals had filed tax contracts with the IRS, with the indictments directly related to the contracts they submitted. 2300 people out of 350 million is six people out of every 1 million. Can you see how problematic it is that most Americans pay a tax they don't owe, with fear being the motive?

### The Formula for Going to Jail

There is a clear, unchanging formula that can put a person in harm's way, even though statistically it's nearly impossible to be charged with a tax crime when dealing with the IRS:

1. Signing a tax return (Form 1040) under penalty of perjury, thereby agreeing that you owe taxes for a given year.

2. Lying about your reported income allows the IRS to prove that you intentionally omitted taxable earnings.

This formula never changes. The problem isn't simply "not paying taxes"—it's filing a contract (your tax return) that legally binds you to the system and then getting caught lying on it.

**The Jurisdiction Trap**

- The moment you sign and file a 1040 form, you are: Agreeing that the federal income tax applies to you (even though it doesn't).
- Placing yourself under the taxing authority of Washington, D.C., and voluntarily submitting to IRS jurisdiction.
- Accepting the risk of criminal penalties if the numbers you report don't match IRS records.

In other words, signing a tax contract under penalty of perjury is more dangerous than not signing at all. People who get into trouble don't go to jail simply for not paying taxes—they go to prison because they voluntarily agreed to the system and then violated its rules. In other words, they actually agreed to go to jail by signing their way into it.

What If I Am Caught for Tax Evasion? This question often arises when someone considers establishing an unincorporated nonprofit association (UNA) and elects to receive money through a tax-exempt entity instead of their Social Security Number (SSN). It's important to understand that tax evasion is different from tax avoidance. Tax evasion occurs only:

- When an individual files a tax contract (1040) with the IRS
- He/she intentionally misreports the numbers on that contract.

Everything in commerce, especially taxation, revolves around the 9-digit Social Security Number assigned to individuals at birth. This number follows a person throughout their life and serves as their financial identifier. It is a birth trust account established by the government as a conduit to conduct business for that baby's lifetime upon a parent's signature on the birth certificate. So, whenever you get a bill in the mail of any kind or if the IRS mails you a letter, they are addressing you as the authorized user of the fictitious birth trust regarding the administration of it. It may help calm fears to know the letter deals with the fiscal accounting of the Social Security trust and can help you respond appropriately.

When someone voluntarily enters into a contract with the IRS by signing a 1040 tax return, they legally obligate their SSN to be subject to the tax. However, suppose a person never uses their SSN to receive income and instead receives money through a tax-exempt Employer Identification Number (EIN) assigned to an entity such as a UNA. In that case, they are not committing tax evasion—they are simply avoiding taxation in a lawful manner. This principle works the same if you had directed money owed to you to your grandmother. Sure, grandma is now responsible, but the point is you can avoid money being paid to your Social Security number anyway you choose to.

Tax avoidance is entirely legal. A person can choose to avoid receiving money under their SSN for the rest of their life without any legal repercussions because you, as an authorized user of the 9-digit social security trust account, can simply decide not to receive money affiliated with it. The IRS's tax evasion claim only applies if an individual voluntarily grants the agency jurisdiction over their SSN by filing tax returns, continues to receive money reported to the SSN, and fails to report it. There are a couple of straightforward solutions:

1. Remove yourself from the system by breaking your contractual relationship with the IRS.

2. Stop signing tax returns, stop reporting money under your SSN, and structure money being received to be lawfully paid to an exempt organization outside of the jurisdiction of the IRS, such as an unincorporated nonprofit association.

If I Receive No More Money, Isn't That a Red Flag? The specific concern stems from the same perceived fear—that "shadowy figure on the wall at the foot of your bed." The IRS is not a school bully lurking in the locker room, waiting to strike the moment you stop receiving income under your Social Security Number (SSN). There is no law requiring you to continuously receive money through your SSN, an LLC, S-Corp, C-Corp, or any other taxable entity. Even if someone once earned millions under their SSN and suddenly reported zero, if the SSN received zero reporting, all that matters is that the accounting matches their system. I know this first-hand—it happened to me. I became a ghost in the game of commerce overnight.

Later in this chapter, I will explain how the IRS functions primarily as an accounting firm. Its system collects third-party reported financial data— income that others have attributed to your SSN. If no one reports income to your SSN, the IRS has no reason to expect a return from you. There is no such thing as a "red flag" when their system registers zero reported income. In fact, the opposite is true—you disappear from the system's radar because, without reported income, no filing requirement exists. The fear of an IRS crackdown in such a situation is simply another illusion, much like the imaginary monster on the wall.

What if I get audited? On the other hand, an audit can only be triggered based on a previously filed tax return where a discrepancy exists between the money reported to the IRS by third parties and the money you personally reported on your return. In other words, an audit is not some random event—it is a systematic review of a filed contract. The IRS is just an accounting firm auditing its own numbers.

The IRS cannot audit a tax year for which no return was filed. The system requires you to first voluntarily submit a signed tax return—essentially a contract admitting that you owe a tax liability. Without this self-submission, there is nothing to audit. No signed contract, agreement, or liability—no audit.

This chapter is dedicated to educating people on how the IRS system honestly operates—through contracts, accounting, and administrative procedures—so that fear can be eliminated.

First and foremost, the IRS functions primarily through contractual agreements, self-assessment, and procedural enforcement. The federal income tax system is rooted in voluntary compliance, meaning that individuals assess and report their own tax liability. This concept was reaffirmed in Flora V. United States (1950), where the Supreme Court stated that "our system of taxation is based upon voluntary assessment and payment, not upon distrain." Yet, millions still end up paying federal income tax due to a misunderstanding of their legal obligations and the nature of IRS procedures.

A major reason so many people file tax returns stems from employer withholding. When you start a job, you fill out a W-4 form. This form authorizes your employer to withhold federal income tax from your paycheck. Essentially, it allows you to "tell" your employer how much of your money should be sent to the IRS. Once they go a year withholding money from their paychecks, they naturally want to file their first tax return to get the money back from what was withheld. The hook word the IRS calls it – "a refund". Ironically, this is exactly how they enter the system in the first place. They would have had a lot more money than just the refund had they stopped the withholdings.

Few people are ever told they can claim "EXEMPT" on the W-4 form, which instructs the employer not to withhold federal taxes. When I got my first job in 1987, nobody explained to me that I was fully exempt from the federal income tax. Had I filed as EXEMPT, my entire paycheck would have been mine, no deductions, no IRS involvement, and no reason to file a tax return that year—or ever. Yet most people unknowingly surrender their freedom the moment they file for a refund.

Once someone files that first return, the system automatically reinforces their participation. Banks, mortgage lenders, credit agencies, and businesses all operate under federal regulations that prioritize IRS compliance. Forms like the W-9, as well as third-party reporting systems such as 1099s and W-2s, create automatic records of who is earning and when. In essence, the IRS has everyone "reporting" on each other, confirming who has money coming in. In some communities, this is called being a "snitch." In the IRS economy, it's just normal business: every January, 1099s and W-2s are mailed out, and the cycle continues.

Another reason the system appears mandatory is the influence of licensed professionals. CPAs, tax attorneys, and enrolled agents are trained exclusively in IRS statutes and procedures—not in challenging the fundamental jurisdiction of the tax system. Their certifications and ability to practice are tied to IRS-recognized licensing bodies, which prohibit them from advising clients to opt out of tax filings. Simply put, their livelihood depends on the continued compliance of taxpayers.

This creates a feedback loop: people file because professionals advise them to, and professionals advise because the system depends on compliance. Meanwhile, most taxpayers never realize that without entering into a voluntary contract, they would not owe the tax in the first place.

By filing a first tax return, individuals essentially declare themselves residents of Washington, D.C. and voluntarily submit to federal taxation. For most, this begins as a teenager with their first job. No one instructs the young worker to claim EXEMPT status, so taxes are automatically withheld. Seeing money withheld from every paycheck, the new worker is lured by the promise of a refund. Filing a 1040 tax return seems like a windfall—free money from the government—but in reality, it is just a tiny portion of what was already taken.

The real consequence is that filing creates a contractual relationship with the IRS. From that moment on, taxpayers unknowingly agree to continue participating in the system, even if they do not legally owe taxes. The system operates as if this contract must be honored indefinitely, unless one consciously chooses to break free.

Once you understand the contractual nature of tax filings, you can make informed choices. The legal method for severing the relationship is through an affidavit known as a "Revocation of Election." This document formally corrects your status and withdraws voluntary participation in the tax system.

Think of it like a divorce—except this breakup is one you'll celebrate, not mourn. By revoking the election, you reclaim financial independence, free yourself from annual filings, and restore the non-taxpayer status you had before signing your first 1040. The IRS treats taxpayers as if they are married to the system, expecting compliance every year. But with a Revocation of Election, you can annul that "marriage" and return to the freedom you had before ever signing a tax contract.

Now, let's talk about how the IRS's robotic accounting system actually operates. Remember, people picture the IRS as a school bully, ready to come knocking on their door the moment they stop filing. But that's not how the system works. The IRS must obtain your consent to establish a tax liability, and they do this through your voluntary act of signing a tax return. If there is no contract filed for a given year, you cannot be accused of owing money—unless you ignore a long series of administrative letters. The system is built on consent, and without a signed agreement, there's nothing for them to enforce.

The IRS operates as a massive, automated accounting system that tracks all financial activity tied to your Social Security number. Every business transaction, real estate sale, or investment you make is reported under the SSN or Employer Identification Number (EIN) linked to it. Banks, investment firms, and other entities automatically send this information to the IRS, feeding the system with a constant data stream.

This system is not some shadowy force targeting individuals—it's simply a mechanized process that categorizes taxpayers based on prior agreements. If your SSN or EIN has received financial reporting, the IRS assumes you have an ongoing contractual relationship with them. And because of that past agreement—your signed tax return—the system assumes you owe tax. The key takeaway? The system operates on consent. If you never signed a contract in the first place, or if you formally revoke it, there's no legal basis for them to claim you owe anything.

### It's an Administrative Process

For years, I made the mistake of ignoring these administrative letters, tossing them in the trash without a second thought. This was before I formally revoked my election and terminated my contractual relationship with the IRS. What I failed to realize back then is that these letters are offers to contract, and if you ignore them for 30 days, the IRS assumes your silence as acceptance of their terms. This kicks off an administrative process that allows them to assess a tax liability against your Social Security account.

It's a catch-22. If you don't file a tax return for a given year for which your social security number has received money, you haven't agreed to owe a tax, meaning they cannot legally assess a liability without your signed 1040 contract. However, if you still have an existing contractual relationship with the IRS—one where you've implicitly agreed to be taxed under Washington, D.C.'s jurisdiction (as the 16th Amendment applies there)— they can continue sending reminder notices. As these letters escalate, their goal shifts: instead of requesting that you voluntarily file, they attempt to use your non-response as consent, ultimately leading to a new administrative approach to enforce the tax.

The IRS follows a structured sequence of letters when attempting to assess a tax liability for a year in which no return has been filed. First, they send a request for a missing return. If ignored, they follow up with a summary of reported income tied to the social security number for that year. If there is still no response, they proceed with what they call a "substitute return." Finally, if the taxpayer continues to remain silent, the process escalates to lien and levy notices, marking the point where the IRS transitions into debt collection mode, actively seeking assets held in accounts linked to the social security number.

The key takeaway? You will see this coming well in advance. This is why it's important not to possess assets tied to your social security number if there exists an existing contractual relationship, as the IRS, like any debt collector, is limited to collecting from the 9-digit number they are targeting. An unincorporated nonprofit association is one of these entities that will never be targeted, and it's not affiliated with a Social Security number. They are a private member association in which you can remain anonymous.

As I mentioned earlier, I learned this the hard way. Early in my discovery process, I ignored the entire sequence of administrative letters over a span of a couple of years, during which the IRS was attempting to assess a tax liability for prior years in which I hadn't filed tax returns. My biggest mistake? Not responding. What I later realized is that the IRS grants a 30-day response window, and if you don't reply, they treat your silence as consent.

When the IRS begins assuming a tax liability, it issues a "Notice of Substitute Return." In this letter, they state that since they haven't heard from you, they will assume a certain amount of income was received in that year. They also warn that if you don't respond within 30 days, they will file a return on your behalf.

As I navigated this administrative gauntlet, I had a significant realization— if I had responded within 30 days with a short reply like "I don't agree," it would have disrupted their process. The IRS operates on an administrative procedure, and any response forces it to slow down and reassess.

Now, let's talk about back taxes. Many people, burdened by past tax liabilities, seek out settlement companies to negotiate with the IRS for a lower balance.

But here's the catch—these settlements come with strings attached. More often than not, part of the agreement requires you to file tax returns for the next five years.

Why does the IRS do this? Simple. They want to keep you locked into the system. By accepting a reduced tax liability, you're essentially signing up for another five years of contractual obligation. It's not about resolving your debt—it's about keeping you in the marriage with the IRS.

In summary, the IRS is not some schoolyard bully waiting to ambush you in the locker room. If you've ever faced aggressive letters, frozen accounts, or personal visits, it's because, at some point, you unknowingly agreed to it. Every action they take stems from a contractual agreement—you either misreported income, failed to balance the books, or didn't challenge their claims by not responding to administrative letters. The IRS is not a law enforcement agency—it's an accounting firm that tracks money that is reported to Social Security numbers and EINs.

One of the simplest ways to sidestep the entire issue is to stop having income reported to your Social Security number in the first place. A straightforward method? Establish an unincorporated nonprofit association (UNA) and allow it to receive assets instead. This removes your personal SSN from the equation, meaning there's no contract for them to enforce—and no "you owe us" letters piling up in your mailbox.

# *Chapter Seven: The Question - And - Answer Approach*

When people first encounter the idea of an unincorporated nonprofit association, they often ask, "What does nonprofit even mean? Is this like a 501(c)(3)? Like a church or a charity?" The confusion is understandable. For most, the word "nonprofit" has been tied exclusively to the realm of religious institutions, soup kitchens, or tax-deductible donation receipts. But in truth, the word carries no legal meaning at all. It is a word that has been designed to cause the brain to think of taxation because the word is linked to an IRS code or statute. A "nonprofit", going by an IRS definition, doesn't mean the organization doesn't make a profit. It is designed to make an exclusive category of tax-exempt entities, by which they attempt to control the gateway of approval by confusing terms. In reality, if you are not under the jurisdiction of Washington, D.C., then nothing regarding the Federal Income tax applies to you or its imposed terms.

The next question almost always follows: "What makes the

association exempt? Why doesn't it have to file a tax return?" To answer that, we have to untangle the web of assumptions people have carried for years. And the most common mistake—one repeated again and again—is that people instinctively turn to the IRS for answers. They search the IRS website.

They scour its publications. They try to decode a system designed not to speak their language.

But this is where the fear takes shape, like that childhood shadow on the wall. It grows only because we assume it holds power over us. The truth is simpler, quieter, and far less terrifying. You do not go to an entity that lacks jurisdiction over you to understand your standing. That would be like consulting Canadian law to resolve a legal issue in Texas—it may be printed in black and white, but it carries no authority over you.

The IRS is not the governing body of your life unless you voluntarily step into its domain. Its rules, its codes, and its forms are all rooted in a specific, narrow jurisdiction. Outside of that boundary, its language is just that— words on a page, devoid of force. When you begin to understand this, the shadow on the wall begins to fade. The figure that once loomed so large shrinks into something harmless. Something powerless. Something that was never about you in the first place.

Once in a while, someone stumbles across a sliver of code during a late-night Google search and suddenly feels the cold breath of doubt crawl up their spine. They read that a nonprofit making over $5,000 is required to file a form, Form 1023 or 1023-EZ. But what they rarely notice, quietly tucked into the fine print, is the condition that governs that requirement: if you want to be recognized by the IRS. That's the catch. That's the bait.

Recognition sounds harmless, official, even comforting. It's the kind of stamp people crave, a sign that what they're doing is legitimate, accepted, and valid. But in legal terms, recognition is a door that opens into someone else's game. Filing that form isn't an obligation; it's a request to enter into a contract.

A voluntary agreement. It's a step into a system that has rules and controls. The truth is, we do not seek recognition because our authority is not drawn from theirs. The association remains private because it remains unregistered, unentangled, and unbound by the rules governing organizations seeking that recognition.

Still, doubt lingers. Fear doesn't always vanish on command. It clings like a shadow, hovering just beyond the periphery of their thoughts. People reach out—some hesitant, others desperate. "What if I'm wrong?" they ask, their voices trembling with uncertainty. "What if I'm missing something important?" That's when I bring them back to what was already said in the previous chapter—fear must be faced, not fed. I tell them, "Let's start with the Loch Ness Monster. Then, we'll talk about Bigfoot. Maybe throw in snakes or a fear of heights. Eventually, we'll get to the IRS."

The humor isn't there to mock their concerns. It's to shrink them. To reframe them, to put them in their proper perspective. The IRS, for many, is a mythic presence—untouchable, omnipotent, a boogeyman lurking in the shadows. Intangible, terrifying, with the power to ruin lives at the stroke of a pen. But myths only hold power when we believe in them. The reality is, most people have never seen the law itself or understood their right granted by the Constitution to be free from a tax by a national government.

They've only heard its echoes: that the IRS can imprison, seize, destroy. What they haven't been shown—what they don't realize—is that the foundation for this power is built on nothing but a whisper of fear. There is no law that explicitly requires them to file a form, especially under the circumstances we're discussing.

That's when I point them to the truth. I reference former IRS agents— seasoned professionals who spent years scouring the depths of tax codes and legal documents, only to discover that the very law they feared didn't exist. These are the same people who, after years of searching, were forced to admit that what had been presented as an undeniable requirement was nothing more than a phantom. The truth begins to sink in. Eyes clear. Breath steadies. The shadow begins to dissolve. It was never real power. Only imagined force. A projection of fear, nurtured by silence and reinforced by ignorance.

What they choose after that moment is theirs. Some may still choose the road of filing, seeking the safety of recognition. Others will see the path that remains open to them—the road of sovereignty, where their actions are governed by their own understanding of the law, not by the whims of an external authority. But at least now, they choose to be awake. With eyes wide open to the truth. Faith, after all, begins where fear once ruled. Once the myth is stripped away, all that remains is the clarity of knowing what is and what isn't. That is the power of understanding.

As I sat down to explain the intricacies of tax exemption to a client, I felt the same sense of purpose that had driven me in countless conversations before. The words, though technical, were simple. The concept was clear, resonating like a steady rhythm in the back of my mind.

Stop using the Social Security number assigned to me from birth.

It's a shift, a simple reallocation, but it holds the power to change everything. When income is no longer tied to that nine-digit number, the reporting stops. The heavy hand of reporting and monitoring lightens. The fear that once lurked in the shadows begins to dissipate.

It's not about wrestling with a mountain of jargon or dissecting endless legal clauses. The key is understanding the flow of money—the freedom that comes when you redirect it through structures designed to protect.

A tax-exempt organization isn't just a tool; it's a vehicle, one that moves income away from the prying eyes of the IRS, one that offers sanctuary without complication. It's as straightforward as it is transformative, like a river changing its course, the pressure lifting as it finds a new channel.

In a world where everything feels bound by the rules of paperwork and fear, this simple concept can feel like a revelation. People don't need to become experts in the language of tax laws to understand them. They just need to realize that there is a clear, direct path that allows them to move with ease through a system designed to trap them. When they realize it, that's when the shift happens. They see the shadow for what it really is—a projection of fear, fed by silence and ignorance.

The more I guide people through this, the more I see the fear begin to melt away. They don't struggle with the technical terms, because they're not what's important. What matters is the underlying idea: take control of the flow, shift the focus, and in doing so, you free yourself from the weight of the system that once seemed all-encompassing.

Industries might vary—some are more complex than others—but

the challenge is the same. It doesn't matter whether you're in tech, retail, or consulting; the structure of your business can be adapted. For those who want to keep their existing framework intact, it's as simple as assigning the ownership of the company to the association. Nothing changes in the day-to-day operations. It's business as usual. For others, they might choose to receive income directly through the new association, bypassing the usual income-reporting channels altogether. Both paths lead to the same destination: tax efficiency, financial protection, and a sense of control over their future.

It's a revelation that cuts through the noise of complicated regulations and charts. With just a small shift, the shadows clear. There's always a solution, always a way to navigate the structure that best suits your needs.

It doesn't matter what industry you're in; the foundation remains the same, and the outcome is the same—freedom from the weight of unnecessary complexity.

There is something powerful about knowing that with just a few strategic moves, you can take the pressure off, release yourself from the grip of a system that once seemed untouchable. It's not about defiance; it's about understanding, about choosing to operate within a framework that empowers, not enslaves. Faith begins where fear once ruled.

The key to this transformation is education. To truly grasp the potential for freedom, to move from fear to confidence, you must first understand the tools at your disposal. Knowledge becomes your armor, and with it, you no longer stand in the shadows of uncertainty. A person who is informed is not a victim of the system; they are its equal. When you know your rights, you walk in them with assurance. You don't question whether you're doing the right thing—you know you are. That's the power of understanding.

Someone once said, "A man who doesn't know his rights doesn't have any." It's a statement that rings with undeniable truth. Rights, freedoms, and the means to protect them don't simply appear—they are claimed, understood, and wielded. Without the knowledge to claim them, you remain vulnerable to forces that would rather you stay ignorant, dependent, and fearful. Education isn't just a tool; it's a form of self-defense.

This journey requires commitment. It's not a single lesson or a one-time workshop. It's a lifetime of unlearning—undoing the years of conditioning, the lies we've been told, and the limitations placed upon us by those who benefit from our ignorance. This is where true empowerment begins: in the quiet unraveling of false beliefs and the replacing of them with the clear, unwavering truth.

To ensure that you stay informed and proactive, we offer ongoing training and regular meetings. This isn't about handing you a set of instructions and sending you on your way. It's about creating a community—a lifelong support system where learning never ends. The world changes, laws evolve, and new strategies emerge. However, the core principle remains the same: knowing how to move within the system while still staying free from its grasp.

Each meeting, each piece of new information, serves to strip away another layer of uncertainty.

Over time, what once felt like a complex and intimidating world becomes clear and navigable. You begin to see opportunities where others see only obstacles, and with that clarity comes the confidence to act—no longer shackled by the fear of what might happen, but empowered by the knowledge of what you can do.

This journey, though long, is worth every step. Because in the end, it's not just about taxes or structures; it's about regaining control, reclaiming your right to operate freely, and knowing that the power you've been seeking has always been within your reach.

# *Chapter Eight: Building A Legacy Of Freedom*

One of the most remarkable visions I had in this journey was that I was never obligated to pay the income tax I had been paying (approximately

$200K annually) legally. Trust me, that was a game-changer. It wasn't just the amount of money saved! While that's a substantial amount of money, what I found more interesting was learning that my financial obligations had been determined based on such long-held assumptions rather than current, applicable laws.

Discovering that most Americans have grown up in a system of deceit about how money, credit, and taxation were an overwhelming revelation that hit me very heavy. In one weekend in Baltimore, Maryland, in September of 2009, I learned the fundamental fraud of the mechanics of our monetary system. The fraud centers on who the Federal Reserve is, how they stole our Country from us, and how they gain our allegiance as a collective whole. Besides taking back our money supply and printing our money again as before 1913, as commissioned by our Constitution, the one thing we can control on an individual level is to eliminate paying a tax that doesn't apply to most Americans living in the 50 republic states.

It isn't just that most Americans do not owe the Federal Income tax that is the heaviest part of the revelation. What is most bothersome is that a share of the Federal Income tax is funneled under the guise of paying down a "national debt", engineered by the international bankers who are the masked men behind the Federal Reserve. They have hijacked our money supply in 1913, and due to monetary policies, they largely impact every aspect of our Country, and due to "taxpayer" allegiance of blindly donating up to a third of their money earnings, they siphon off due to immense evil in the world.

If the money went back to support our local communities in our counties and States, then that would be fine. But this is not the case. Sales tax, property tax, gas tax, road tax, and many other taxes support your local police departments, fire departments, build schools and parks, and many other community needs, such as road infrastructure. The money that the IRS collects in the name of a "Federal Income Tax" goes to both fund a cause in Washington, D.C. that is nearly always not in the best interests of the republic 50 states but rather under false premises going for other causes that the international bankers influence, such as wars, and fund many immoral things too disturbing to mention. They stage false flags and then present Americans with a solution to the problem they created. The lion's share goes directly to the international bankers in an effort to actually kill off the population. Since this statement is too difficult to lay out agendas such as 911 and COVID, I'll just let the reader pray and do their own research on these things.

I can only hope I've been able to reach a few souls with my story in the book and the actions that I've taken to find a safe and legal way to eliminate income tax. Once you realize you never even owed the tax from birth, unless you've worked as a federal employee, then it will be easier to see the agenda behind keeping Americans in the dark and allowing tax professionals with licenses to propagate the false commitment to people.

Waking up to this reality was way bigger than me. I have found a mission to help people wake up to a cause worthy of the same battle the Founding Fathers fought, called the Revolutionary War between 1775 and 1783. They fought a standing army to break free from a tax that did not go to their local colonies. We only fight ourselves in the waking-up process. Albeit it is a herculean effort to wake some people who just do not want to face reconciling a lifetime of deception when presented with this information, for those who do want to know the truth, you do not face losing your life in a battle. You face a simple administrative process.

Deliverance from a lifetime of a mind molded around a system of taxation is not an overnight process. Just like the Revolutionary War was not won overnight. But those who stayed the course tasted a freedom that echoed for generations. You will face doubt, and at times metaphorically you will 'look over your shoulder' so to speak as if somebody is chasing you. But remember, the battle is no longer physical. You are not facing bullets or cannons. You are facing paperwork, patience, and a process.

You see, this winning battle strategy is grounded in law. So, when you make a legal move to revoke your standing as a taxpayer and set up a legal entity to operate in, outside of the confines of your social security number, then you can never have personal liability. Simply stop volunteering. George Washington, Thomas Jefferson, and James Madison would be proud of you winning this personal battle because the same powers behind the scenes that they found physically, you will gain victory over mentally and emotionally.

The hardest part is to take the first step. The road of traveling by faith always begins with taking a first step toward truth, and the next steps will then be revealed one at a time. The rewards last longer than the mental discomfort of unlearning old beliefs. When you see and experience truth, how can you turn back? The system wants you to break down a little, to get stressed or just exhausted. Paving a new income tax-free path means living a life free from the trap that was set before you were born.

By doing what you should, you create something your children and grandchildren will operate in a part of, something they will enjoy, and something that is based on real freedom: freedom of thought, freedom of transport, and the freedom to work outside the old system meant to squeeze you dry.

Those who choose to stay the course cross a threshold that very few know of. Once you establish your exempt entity through an unincorporated nonprofit association, the benefits are not just financial; they are spiritual and mental. You are no longer a volunteer in a system built on fear and your ignorance of how it functions.

www.ingramcontent.com/pod-product-compliance
Lightning Source LLC
LaVergne TN
LVHW011519200926
848484LV00001B/69